In celebration of
our friendship!
Happy Birthday,
Norma

# You Bring the Confetti

# You Bring the Confetti

# the

# Confetti

## Luci Swindoll

**WORD BOOKS**
**PUBLISHER**
**WACO, TEXAS**

**A DIVISION OF**
**WORD, INCORPORATED**

YOU BRING THE CONFETTI

**Library of Congress Cataloging in Publication Data:**

Swindoll, Luci, 1932–
  You bring the confetti.

  1. Joy—Religious aspects—Christianity.   I. Title.
BV4905.2.S93   1986      242        86–13332
ISBN 0–8599–0527–3

67898   BKC   987654321

*Printed in the United States of America*

To
Marilyn Meberg
in celebration of
our companionship


In love, in faith unbroken dwell,
Friends radiant and inseparable!
Rupert Brooke

# CONTENTS

# ACKNOWLEDGMENTS

It has been suggested by Dr. Alan Loy McGinnis, author of the bestseller, *The Friendship Factor,* that people should use every success as an excuse for celebration. I couldn't agree more. He says when a task is finished and there's a sense of achievement, celebration is in order.

So, let's celebrate! The manuscript of this book has been written, typed, and put into print by my publisher. I'm ready to throw confetti. Better yet—let's have a party. I'll invite a few honored guests. I must invite Marilyn Meberg, of course, to whom this book is dedicated. For months she patiently listened to chapter after chapter, offering input, feedback, and constant encouragement. She'll be the one in the very bright party hat labeled, "Friendship knows no limit. I've heard it all!"

Also on the guest list is Nancy King. With her marvelous skills at the typewriter and her eagle eye, Nancy enhanced this manuscript immeasurably. Not only that, but she did it in record time. I mailed her my work from Los Angeles to Washington, D.C., where she lives, and in one week she had it back in my hands in completed form. Her party hat will read, "Fastest fingers in town." She will be among those honored!

Ernie Owen, Vice President and Editorial Director of Word, Inc., will be there because were it not for his invitation, *You Bring The Confetti* would not have been published. And I'll invite his editing staff as well. They will all be easily recognized with labeled hats: "We made it happen."

But, most of all, my guest list will also include a very, very special person: YOU. By choosing this book, you have demonstrated a certain measure of trust in my work, and for that, I truly thank you. This celebration party is for you . . . all of you, and my gift to you is the message of this book. May it be fun to read and an encouragement in your life.

I'll know who you are at the party. The label on your hat will say, "I brought the confetti. Get on with the celebration."

# Introduction

Brace yourself! This little piece of information may come as a shock. When I was a kid I used to make up Bible verses. Oh, it's not that there weren't enough verses already in the Bible—my brothers and I used to say there were trillions. It's that more often than not they didn't cover exactly what I wanted them to. So, I decided with a little creativity and imagination I could come up with a few "scriptures" to better fit my circumstances, to meet more of my needs. They wouldn't be nearly as sacred, but they would suit my situations more precisely.

Since I have always been one who loved words, I was fascinated with the lofty language of the Bible. It *sounded* holy—all those *thees* and *thous* and *verilies.* So with elevated and sublime syntax, I began to compose verses. I had verses about school . . . verses about playmates . . . ballgames . . . relatives . . . clothes . . . music . . . my brothers (very choice verses about my brothers) . . . and my favorite subject: parties! I loved parties, and I never understood why there weren't any

11

holy words on the subject. And there was nothing written on celebrations either—not to my knowledge.

How could all those prophets and apostles have been so monotonous as to have never attended a party? Or if they had, why had they not written about it? That wouldn't do.

My best verse along this line came to me one afternoon on the way home from school:

> Verily, verily I say unto you: thou shalt find a party at the end of this street. Turn not to the right nor the left, but direct your steps toward it. Great will be your fun upon arrival. Walk ye in haste.

Doesn't that have a magic ring to it? Once I committed that little verse to memory and used it with regularity, I cannot tell you how it lightened my step and brightened my outlook on an otherwise long, hot, dusty, two-mile walk home. This was another favorite:

> Thou sluggard! (*I always loved that descriptive term.*) Get ye up. Throw thou a party. Today calls for a celebration.

Sometimes I would add a little tag on the end, "Git at it!" just for snap and a strengthening effect—much like "God forbid" in the real Scriptures.

You must understand in the core of my heart and soul I was aware that my simple verses were powerless to effect real change. They had no authenticity or inerrancy. I knew that. But they were heartfelt. What they lacked in credibility I made up for in gullibility. And it was amazing what happened to my behavior and my attitude as a result.

If I was low, somehow these homespun homilies cheered me up, lifted me, and brought me out of what was otherwise troubling me or making me feel deprived in my spirit. If I was without a playmate, the sheer suggestion of one (the perfect one, naturally) appearing at the next turn of the road gave me *oomph* to keep going. If I had nothing exciting to anticipate that evening, making up a verse about an upcoming festival, party, or gala event created something to which I looked forward. It changed my mood and lifted my soul. It gave me a reason to celebrate life and put the burdens of the real world out of my mind. I do it even now as an adult. I don't make up Scriptures anymore, but I do look for ways to celebrate living. I call this mental activity "giving myself a perk."

Have you ever done that for your soul? Have you looked at the hour before you, with its myriad demands, plans, concerns, and problems and asked God, in the midst of all that, to give you a perk—just for the love of life . . . no other reason? The highest and most desirable state of the soul is to praise God in celebration for being alive. Without perks our lives are easily lost in the world of money, machines, anxieties, or inertia. Our poor, splendid souls! How they fight for food! They have forgotten how to celebrate. They have forgotten how to request little perks. Our hurried, stressful, busy lives are unquestionably the most dangerous enemy of celebrating life itself. Somehow, we must learn how to achieve momentary slowdowns, and request from God a heightened awareness of the conception that life is a happy thing, a festival to be enjoyed rather than a drudgery to be endured. Life is *full* of perks if we train our souls to perceive them, ". . . a thousand tiny things from which one can weave a bright necklace of little pleasures for one's life."

About two years ago I was driving down a rain-swept street in Long Beach, California on an errand from my office. It was cold, the day was dreary, the sky was overcast, I couldn't find the address I was seeking and my spirit was out of sorts. I hadn't wanted to leave the comfort of a warm office but I had no choice. You know how it goes—the demands of duty. As I was driving along, fretting about a problem that was sapping my emotional energy, I said to God, "Lord, would You please give me a perk? Some little something to lift my spirit? Doesn't have to be big. Doesn't have to be flashy. Just do something creative to cheer me up and to remind me that I'm glad I'm alive. I'd appreciate that very much."

At that moment I turned the corner, looked to my left and there in the cab of a pickup truck sat two clowns. They were fully decked out in clown regalia, complete with red woolen yarn hair, big bow ties, painted faces, and each holding a helium-filled balloon. As I looked at them, they simultaneously turned, looked at me, and flashed toothless grins from ear to ear. What a unique answer to prayer. I absolutely *loved* it, and all alone in my car I yelled, *"Alright!!* Great perk, Lord. What an idea. How clever You are. Who would ever have thought of two clowns in a pickup?" For the rest of the day I envisioned those cheerfully dressed fellows and how they appeared out of nowhere in the twinkling of an eye. And I smiled again and again and again.

That's the whole idea. Life is full of subtle, unsuspected, hidden perks, ready to make their presence known at the turn of a corner to cheer us, to lift us, to change our attitudes, to give our souls a reason to celebrate. Don't miss them. Don't let them pass by unnoticed. That would be a shame and a significant loss to your emotional and spiritual growth. Celebrate those perks one by one, day after day. Celebrate living!

Throw thou a party and invite me. I'll bring a couple of clowns I know. You bring the confetti!

# 1
# Celebrating Now

## SAVORING THE MOMENT

Several months ago I read a rather insignificant article in the newspaper entitled "What Makes for Happiness?" Under that broad heading were these pithy words from comedian George Burns: "Love what you're doing and don't retire . . . I would rather be a failure at something I love than a success at something I hate." Like George Burns, we each have our own special formula for happiness in our day-to-day living, both at work and at play. The ingredients we need to enjoy life may be anything from a pleasant working environment to good literature, good food, good company, or good entertainment—or any combination of the above.

It is true that to enjoy a full life, one that is not cynical, embittered, remorseful, or impoverished, each person must come up with his or her own formula for living happily. *What makes life fun? What makes it rich? What keeps it interesting and worth the investment of energy over the long haul?* Those are questions we each ask ourselves and ones which only we can answer. As the artist protagonist declared in a novel I was reading recently, "We need so little for happiness when we grow older and begin freezing down at the feet: eight to ten hours' work a day, a cool and tasty drink, a half pound of bread, a little love, and of course warmth and good weather."

Like George Burns, this man is trying to prescribe a code of living which states that in order to enjoy and sustain a feeling of happiness, harmony, and health, we need to experience the feeling of being alive. Sir William Osler said that we make our own happiness: "We are here to add what we can *to,* not to get what we can *from* Life." We must seek that which enhances our beings—body, mind, spirit. Human nature looks for that which pleases both our logical and sensitive sides. We want to think and feel. Even though these components for good health do not necessarily have to be comprehensible, they do have to move us. They have to give us something! That which makes us happy must have the capacity to give us an overall feeling of pleasure, momentary or fleeting though it may be. In fact, because it is just that—short-lived—it provides even more enjoyment because we know it will not last. Like stolen fruit, it is ours until it is repossessed and whisked away. The very joy of it derives its magic from its transience.

Let's look at it another way. To experience happiness we must train ourselves to live in this moment, to savor it for what it is, not running ahead in anticipation of some future date nor lagging behind in the paralysis of the past. With wholeness and sensitivity we must live in the here and now. "But what if I don't like the here and now?" you ask. "What if my present moment is one of disappointment or impairment or heartache? How then do I savor that moment?" Good questions. And the answers reside in the first and most profound principle for the art of savoring life: *Pleasure lies in the heart, not in the happenstance.* Our circumstances may be dreadful and riddled with reasons for discouragement or sorrow, but that doesn't mean those moments are utterly devoid of happiness. The first necessity for happiness is freedom from the tyranny of time.

I well remember my father's years of failing health prior to his death five years ago. It was a stage of life that had a face and character all its own. My mother had died seven or eight years earlier, and Dad, vibrant in his youth and always enjoying life to its fullest, hated being old and alone. He often verbalized his lack of enjoyment with the company of other white-haired folks. "They're too old," he'd say, yet he was no younger than they. With the passing of time, which lay heavily upon Daddy's hands, my brother Chuck and I elected to put him in a convalescent home—a place where the growing needs of the aged were cared for by professionals. Being rather passive and docile by nature, Daddy rarely complained about this arrangement, but it was obvious he did not enjoy his domestic circumstances nor the inevitability of aging that drove him there. However, with resignation he often admitted, "The worst thing about growing old is to feel your body decaying and not be able to do anything about it." (I cannot tell you the times I have thought about that statement since my father's death, especially as *I* grow older.)

In Daddy's declining years, he experienced infirmity. He no longer trusted his own senses or powers. Walking, which was at one time a treat, became difficult and wearisome. He suffered various disabilities and weakening of the senses, the flagging of bodily organs and functions. This became Daddy's constant state. It was the inescapable reality of his life. And it brought the entire family much sadness and personal grief.

But we refused to settle into that mindset. It became my responsibility and joy to find ways to cheer Daddy. He was capable of doing this for himself, but oftentimes I played a part that gave meaning to his life. I would buy him a new outfit—trousers, shirt, tie, sweater— and take them to him. I would shave him, dress him in his newly purchased clothes, and together we'd walk down the hall of that convalescent home as he preened in his new attire. Loving the praise from the others whom he had earlier labeled "too old," Daddy would smile at them, pass them by, then we'd go out "on the town." He and I would have dinner together at a local restaurant, chatting and laughing aimlessly about any number of things. We'd relive old times, looking again and again at the treasure of pictures Daddy carried in his memory. Many of these friends and times no longer existed on earth, but they went on living within him. They belonged to him. They provided him with company many an evening over dinner. Together Daddy and I entreated their presence into our conversation. They literally and unknowingly entertained us both.

On occasion, Dad would relive his working years— decades he had stormed through driven by ambition, dreams, tension, fulfillment, or disappointment. He took time to recall those experiences and we talked of them at length. When it became too painful or too much of a hassle for him to bodily leave the quarters in which he lived, we'd savor our moments there. Because there was little or nothing to enjoy in Daddy's real world, he found his happiness outside of reality. We'd talk of momentary remembrances that always delighted him. Then, when even that became difficult I would sit with Dad, smile at him, receive his smiles or winks, feed him, hold his hand, tell him jokes—anything to lift him from the reality that was full of pain. We'd talk of Jesus, of Daddy's homegoing to be with the Lord and with Mother. These became deep and personal moments of sharing.

The point I am making here is that, regardless of life's realism, Dad managed to mentally rise above his physical circumstances. He savored moments. He celebrated the *now* within the confines of severe struggles. He counted blessings, divorced from immediate heartaches, even to the end when he gave up his life. The trick to doing this was that pleasure was hidden in Daddy's heart, not in his happenstance.

A second vital lesson the celebration of the moment teaches is that *time is for spending, not saving.* Where did we ever get the idea that by saving time we somehow have it stashed away in a hidden bank account and one day will be able to spend it all? Do we really believe that those extra minutes, hours, days, weeks, months, and years are lying there earning interest? We're planning to spend all that when everything is right . . . when everything is orderly . . . when the kids are grown . . . when the bills are paid . . . when the house is furnished . . . when we have enough. Well, that will only happen when time stands still, and take it from a fifty-three-year-old: Time is *never* going to stand still—not for any of us at any age or at any station in life. It's going to move right along and we're going to move with it whether we're ready or not.

For some reason, the favorite pastime of the twentieth century efficient human being is to find a new way to save time. Isn't that true? Our lives are full of such things as the pressure cooker, the microwave oven, the calculator, the Concorde jet, the speed reader, the one-minute manager. Why? Why must we insist on saving the valuable stuff of which this life is made? We surely can't spend it in the next one. Will Rogers wrote, "Half our life is spent trying to find something to do with the time we have rushed through life trying to save." We simply *cannot* save time like we do pennies in a jar for some rainy day.

Don't get me wrong. I'm just as guilty as the next proficiency seeker, and I hate it in myself. That's why I can write on the subject. I know about it from experience. I'm constantly searching for ways to save time. My most commonly voiced complaint is, "Where is all that time I saved? How am I *ever* going to get all this done?" Ask my friends—they'll tell you. I remember verbalizing to a group of friends last winter, "I've now got Christmas down to a science. I've decided to shop by mail order catalogue." I confessed I hated it in myself. So why do I say such things? Because I forget. I forget that time is for *spending,* not *saving.* It's for filling with happiness. It's for savoring, moment by moment. As Philip Doddridge once said, "Let us live while we live."

One of our basic problems in time saving is that in our effort to shorten unpleasant duties (like defrosting the refrigerator), we shorten the pleasant ones as well (like dining with our friends). We try to get mealtime down to a science. Or we wait for a special occasion to celebrate. Again, we forget that everyday occurrences can be special occasions. As the adage says, "The time to be happy is now."

The fact of this truth was never brought home to me more poignantly than in the following article from the Sunday *Los Angeles Times,* dated April 14, 1985. When I read it I could hardly believe my eyes. It perfectly captures my reason and philosophy for celebrating life now:

## What Are We Waiting For?

My brother-in-law opened the bottom drawer of my sister's bureau and lifted out a tissue-wrapped package.

"This," he said, "is not a slip. This is lingerie." He discarded the tissue and handed me the slip. It was exquisite; silk, handmade and trimmed with a cobweb of lace. The price tag with an astronomical figure on it was still attached.

"Jan bought this the first time we went to New York, at least eight or nine years ago. She never wore it. She was saving it for a special occasion. Well, I guess this is the occasion."

He took the slip from me and put it on the bed with the other clothes we were taking to the mortician. His hands lingered on the soft material for a moment, then he slammed the drawer shut and turned to me.

"Don't ever save anything for a special occasion. Every day you're alive is a special occasion."

I remembered those words through the funeral and the days that followed when I helped him and my niece attend to all the sad chores that follow an unexpected death. I thought about them on the plane returning to California from the Midwestern town where my sister's family lives. I thought about all the things that she hadn't seen or heard or done. I thought about the things that she had done without realizing that they were special.

I'm still thinking about his words, and they've changed my life. I'm reading more and dusting less. I'm sitting on the deck and admiring the view without fussing about the weeds in the garden. I'm spending more time with my family and friends and less time in committee meetings.

Whenever possible, life should be a pattern of experience to savor, not endure. I'm trying to recognize these moments now and cherish them.

I'm not "saving" anything; we use our good china and crystal for every special event—such as losing a pound, getting the sink unstopped, the first camellia blossom.

I wear my good blazer to the market if I feel like it. My theory is if I look prosperous, I can shell out $28.49 for one small bag of groceries without wincing.

I'm not saving my good perfume for special parties; clerks in hardware stores and tellers in banks have noses that function as well as my party-going friends'.

"Someday" and "one of these days" are losing their grip on my vocabulary. If it's worth seeing or hearing or doing, I want to see and hear and do it now.

I'm not sure what my sister would have done had she known that she wouldn't be here for the tomorrow we all take for granted. I think she would have called family members and a few close friends. She might have called a few former friends to apologize and mend fences for past squabbles. I like to think she would have gone out for a Chinese dinner, her favorite food. I'm guessing—I'll never know.

It's those little things left undone that would make me angry if I knew that my hours were limited. Angry because I put off seeing good friends whom I was going to get in touch with—someday. Angry because I hadn't written certain letters that I intended to write—one of these days. Angry and sorry that I didn't tell my husband and daughter often enough how much I truly love them.

I'm trying very hard not to put off, hold back, or save

anything that would add laughter and luster to our lives.

And every morning when I open my eyes I tell myself that it is special.[1]

By Ann Wells

There is a third reason that living in the present moment is a contribution to our prescription for happiness. It is the constant realization that as long as we are on this earth, *this is all there is.* There is no alternative to this life. The world does not offer permanency. Life is transitory and temporal, characterized by changes, modifications, unpredictableness, flux, and alterations. Nevertheless, it is made up of little moments of *now* all added together to constitute the whole of life, a pattern of experience to savor. Those special, savored moments of fun, reflection, happiness, and pleasure give us a tiny taste of what eternity with Christ will one day be like.

In line with that thought, the deepest value of the savored moment is that it offers something to our lives even greater than pleasure. It's a bit hard to explain, but let me try in this way: Imagine something simple that brings to you a fleeting moment of joy—perhaps a bird singing merrily in a tree, the playful antics of a cat, a perfectly formed strawberry, colorful fireworks against a darkened sky, or a beautiful, smiling child who reminds you of your own erstwhile youth and innocence—anything that produces pleasure in your thoughts.

As you view these things in your mind's eye—the bird, the cat, the strawberry, the fireworks, the child—remember that they are "things of a day." They have only a moment to give you joy because they are temporal. They have one single moment—that present moment. Let's call it "your" moment.

But what if that special moment had the capability

of lasting into eternity? You would look at it differently, wouldn't you? Perhaps with a colder eye you'd say to yourself, "I can savor this anytime. It doesn't have to be right now. It doesn't even have to be today." But because you realize that the beautiful things upon the horizon of your view are perishable and cannot last forever, you look at them with more than a feeling of pleasure and momentary happiness. You look at them with love and compassion as well because you are afraid that in a few seconds it will all be over. And the inexorable fact of life is that it *will* be over. But here's the secret: The happiness and fear go together and *that* is what makes your moment more beautiful and meaningful than if it lasted longer. The coupling of those two ingredients makes that moment more than just a simple pleasure. It makes it a memory of sustaining and everlasting satisfaction.

Savoring's very best gift to us, therefore, comes because joy and sorrow merge together as one. In that way, *the fine art of celebrating life gives us the opportunity to appreciate both the temporal and the eternal at the same moment.*

We too are temporal and eternal at the same instant. Our days on this earth are prescribed by transitory moments we call *time*. But one day time is going to run out, whether we are ready or not, and eternity is going to begin.

Five hundred years before the birth of Christ, Greek poet Pindar phrased it this way:

> We are things of a day. What are we? What are we not? The shadow of a dream is man, no more. But when the brightness comes, and God gives it, there is a shining of light on men, and their life is sweet.

Life *is* sweet, sweet enough to be lived fully now. But it's even sweeter when we realize that we can walk in the brightness of God's light as it shines upon us, both now and through eternity.

Sometimes, for a change of pace, I go through the day savoring the idea of eternity. Of course I don't really know exactly what heaven will be like, but that's okay. There are numerous Bible verses telling me about it and I have a picture of it in my mind. I know it will be wonderful. I know it will exceed even my best imaginations. And I know it will never end. That fact alone blows me away! I can't think about it too long because my finite mind can't comprehend it.

So, just for fun, I carry in my billfold two fortune cookie "prophecies" I love. I have saved them for years as reminders to celebrate both the here and now and the up and coming. One says,

A LITTLE MADNESS, A LITTLE KINDNESS,
MAKES FOR HAPPINESS

And the other says,

AN INHERITED TREASURE AWAITS YOU

We all have a prescription for happiness. Mine includes a hearty laugh, a dear friend, a Bach concerto or two, and a moment to savor. And as I live up to that prophecy of "a little madness, a little kindness," I keep in mind that my inherited treasure awaits me. Then I *really* celebrate!

# 2
# Celebrating

# Birthdays

GROWING
OLDER
JOYFULLY

I thrive on any excuse for a party. And birthdays seem to be one of the best excuses of all! I love birthdays—mine or anyone else's. *Everybody* loves birthdays. By that I mean we love the celebration. What we don't like is adding candles to the cake. Nobody loves growing old.

Generally speaking, birthdays denote aging. And while that is inevitable, it's a fact we'd rather ignore. I know. Some days I look in the mirror and say to the face staring back at me, "You're surely not taking *that* on the street today, are you? Look at you. You look awful—all those wrinkles. Think there's time for a face lift before work?"

The painful truth is that while I feel pretty much the same on the inside as I did ten years ago, my physical body has changed radically. "Swiftly changing time, which flies across man's face" has taken my youth. I wear glasses full-time now instead of part-time and, on occasion, have to remove them to see things. My skin, once taut and tan, is now loose and mottled. (I often wonder what it would be like if I didn't use all those creams.) My hearing isn't quite what it used to be, and remembering is often worse than hearing itself. The list goes on and on. As I frequently say to young friends of mine, "I'm no different than I was at your age except everything I have now is either lower or has fallen off." The inexorable sands of time. The unrelenting process of aging. That dreaded cycle of life.

Sages through the ages have offered advice on how to stay young, to make those multiplied birthdays worth anticipating. Now that I am older, I, too, offer advice to any passerby who pauses long enough to listen. People often ask me if it was earth shattering to turn fifty, and I can easily and readily answer, "No." I don't mind being in my fifties. My most difficult decade change, by far, was turning thirty. I thought the earth would open and swallow me. I was reading Sophia Loren's book the other day, *Women & Beauty*, a book that grew out of her experiences as she was looking back from the age of fifty. What comforted me the most was when she confessed that she, too, had trouble turning thirty. Her sentiment expresses a great deal of my thought:

For me, and I think for many women, thirty was the most difficult birthday. At this age your youth is definitely behind you. You may do wonderful things, but no one will ever again say of you, "Yes, and she's so young too!" You have to begin to take responsibility as an adult. You also have to look at your personal life and see if the direction you are moving in is the right one . . . at thirty you begin to realize that fresh beginnings are not always awaiting you. The past is with you to stay, for better or worse.[1]

Those were precisely some of my feelings and uncertainties when my thirtieth birthday came, eons ago. I remember thinking, "Luci, kid, you now have a viable past. You are a responsible adult. Some of the things you always dreamed of doing—like that journey to the center of the earth—you know now you'll never do. What do you *really* want to do with your life? You *are* growing older!"

Before that day I can truthfully say the process of aging was of little or no concern to me. But when I hit thirty and heard, "Happy Birthday! You are now thirty!" I had real misgivings about the word "happy." I did some very deep soul searching and had to realize there was no going back. Until that time all I had done in my youth, for the most part, was suffer the torments of my individuation—the painful process of becoming *me*. But rarely, if ever, did I consider the inevitability of growing old. Suddenly, comprehending I was indeed a responsible adult at thirty, the reality of going forward was my only option.

When I finally recovered from that passage, I consciously set about to make birthdays truly happy occasions—barring ill health, unavoidable conflicts, and possible setbacks that were mine to bear from the hand of God. In other words, I determined from age thirty forward to intentionally celebrate birthdays in a memorable manner to the degree that I was able, thus discovering the fact that life is the joy, not the burden, of aging. This conscious act gave me tremendous insight into the value of making birthdays unforgettable occasions.

To have a happy birthday takes two basic ingredients: creativity of what isn't and acceptance of what is. The creativity is what I call the ideal; the acceptance is the real. But a stronger emphasis can't be placed on one more than the other. They go hand in hand, fitting together perfectly. The idea of a joyful birthday is more than the passing from one year to another. It is a special day to be reminded that one is glad to be alive, no matter what age.

When we sing the song "Happy Birthday to you . . ." we are expressing the wish for the recipient to have a good day of fun, festivity, a bit of craziness, and above all, a chance to let his hair down. "Don't be serious today," we are saying, "be off the wall, because this is *your* day to celebrate." We need to do that for our own birthdays as well as for others. I try to squeeze every ounce of celebration possible into that day, beginning with singing "Happy Birthday" to myself.

Quite often on the natal day of a friend or relative, if they are not available for celebration, I do some tiny perk for them, in their honor. You, too, have special friends. So the next time a birthday rolls around, show them just how special they are. Give them a phone call and sing birthday greetings at an odd hour. Send flowers or a card. Mail a cassette tape. Offer a particular prayer to the Lord in their behalf, thanking God for their life and asking Him to provide an extraordinary day of fun. And, if at all possible, give a personally chosen gift—preferably gift-wrapped. Sometimes, if an individual is very meaningful in my life, I will do all of the above at different times during the day.

Even for my parents, both of whom are with the

Lord, I do something commemorative in their honor. On my mother's birthday last year, I thought about her and how special she had been to me. On impulse, I pushed back from the breakfast table, found a small birthday candle in the cabinet, stuck it into my boiled egg, lighted it, turned off the kitchen lights, and with lifted coffee cup I sang, ". . . happy birthday, dear Mother, happy birthday to you." Maybe that sounds weird. Admittedly, it is out of the ordinary—but I'm glad, because my mother, too, was out of the ordinary. Those few moments spent for her, on her birthday, reminded me again of the values she instilled in me for life. Much of what I am today I owe to her. I am the product of her love and devotion to praying for me, her encouragement, her emphasis on the arts and upon spiritual training. That simple moment of remembrance was created out of what isn't. It took no extra time or money; it just took a few moments to think of her. And it provided enrichment and gratitude throughout my whole day as I thought back on those wonderful memories I relived that morning.

Creatively speaking, one can be quite elaborate with one's plans. I have celebrated birthdays (my own or others) at the beach, on a sailboat, in the mountains, at a dude ranch, in fancy restaurants, in the park, in countless homes, in the desert, on an airplane, in a hospital, and even in a rented hearse we named Patty, for "Patty Hearse." I've decorated scores of cakes, small-scale models of everything from St. Peter's Basilica to La Scala Opera House. I've handmade cards, painted fancy kites, and draped rooms, chairs, tables, and automobiles with streamers, balloons, and crepe paper for birthday parties. I've written limericks and poetry and songs, done the soft-shoe, made up tricks, and hidden behind trees, rocks, pillars, and in the wings for a surprise. I've dressed in masks and costumes, and even flown across the country to express my love to a friend or a family member on his or her birthday . . . just for the fun of it. I've bought meals, cooked meals, and had meals catered—breakfast, lunch, or dinner—for such an occasion. And, I have loved it *all*, madly! I cannot, and will not, go through life without having fun. You shouldn't either.

Friends remember a zany party I once threw to celebrate the fortieth birthday of one of my favorite stars, Barbra Streisand. Of course my relationship with Barbra Streisand is probably much like yours—nonexistent. But I love her singing, her humor, and her wonderful acting, and am probably one of her most enthusiastic fans. Besides, I love any reason to celebrate. So I invited twenty of my closest friends to help me wish Barbra a happy birthday.

What a night to remember! I decorated my apartment with colorful streamers, confetti, crepe paper, giant Streisand posters, and dozens of balloons. A huge chocolate cake read "Barbra's 40th—The Main Event" and was decorated with forty candles. We played charades with her movie and song titles, listened to her record albums, quizzed each other with Streisand trivia questions, and even passed around a "guest book" in which we all wrote birthday greetings to Barbra. Throughout the evening phone calls came from either the envious uninvited or the inviteds who just couldn't make it. Although the guest of honor probably never knew about our party, it was indeed one of my favorite birthday celebrations—and one I'll certainly never forget! Dare to be creative! There are thousands of reasons out there to celebrate, even if it's just the joy of being alive!

How well I recall a marvelously fun birthday celebration for my dear friend Kurt. It was just one of dozens of celebrations we have had in our twenty-two years of friendship. I invited him over for a different kind of celebration, one which I called "A Private Birthday Treasure Hunt." In the card I handed to him at the outset were written directions he was to follow which led him all over my apartment, as well as out of doors, to find various presents. Beginning with the card, he received clues for each stop as he went along. The note took him to one of his favorite poetry books, and from there, to other notes all over the place: between the heddles on my weaving loom, under the strings of my guitar, inside the tea canister, behind a bust of Michelangelo, in a picnic basket, stuck to a cutting board, written on the underside of a jigsaw puzzle piece, on the bathroom mirror, in the oven, hanging on the clock pendulum, on the handle of a vegetable brush, under the mattress in my bedroom, back to a second favorite book, and finally under the hood of my car. Along the way there were brightly wrapped gifts (some of which were handmade), gales of laughter, a few tears, some hugs, and many kisses. On the final gift I had attached this note: "My very best wishes for a happy year ahead, Kurt, and many more to come. We must *always* celebrate together. Not only birthdays, but the *joy of living!*"

A few years ago, a creative, talented, and thoughtful friend named Cyndi gave me a unique birthday celebration. Complete with fried chicken, potato salad, relishes, homemade rolls, and birthday cake, she spread out a quilt, put a vase of flowers in the center, and provided a beautiful picnic—on my living room rug. This was only made *more* complete with the background music, a hodge-podge recording made up of Jean-Pierre Rampal, Alexandre Lagoya, and Claude Bolling in *Picnic Suite,* another of Cyndi's several creative gifts. So unique. And so *fun.*

What makes a birthday happy lies in the creativity

brought into play. It doesn't take a lot of money, and it often doesn't take much time or energy (although it can, of course, include a great deal of all three). The key lies in one's ability to get out of one's self and think of the one being honored, the ability to remember him or her in a special or imaginative way by providing what was not there before. That aspect of a birthday means the *world* to the recipient and, in reflecting upon it or in telling about it to others, believe me, all the colorful and enriching details will be remembered because "somebody cared that much about *me.*"

If you're alone, do it for yourself. Shortly before my own birthday one year, I found a treasure on sale at the posh Dallas store, Neiman-Marcus. A beautiful and expensive collection of antique Spanish lithographs caught my eye. Although the book of lithographs cost an exorbitant amount of money (even on sale), it was my birthday and I figured I deserved it. Besides, the drawings were absolutely exquisite and "something I could not live without." When I told the clerk they were for a birthday present (they probably appeared to be a fairly reasonably priced gift from such a store as Neimans), she inquired, "Would you like them giftwrapped?"

"Oh, absolutely!" I answered unhesitatingly.

I brought the decorated present home and set it in my living room where I admired it for days. On Saturday, my birthday, I got up, got dressed, put on some makeup, and made a pot of fresh-ground coffee. Then I gingerly unwrapped my special gift and once again enjoyed what I had bought. It took hours. I carefully, scrutinizingly inspected and admired all thirty-six lithographs, giving my soul, mind, and emotions a time of rich celebration. Unforgettable! Every now and then, for fun, I make a pot of coffee, pour myself a cup, sit down with that wonderful book, and look at those beautiful, colorful lithographs again. I could have taken the box home from Neimans and not gone to the trouble of having it gift-wrapped but then I would have denied myself that added joy. Why should I? I'm worth it. This way, the fun and excitement started the moment I began to anticipate the unveiling of those precious drawings on my birthday. I created *for myself* a happy occasion. I gave myself a perk!

To grow older joyfully also means to accept what is. This implies we determine to live with the reality that says we are truly the age we are, to date. Any age is beautiful because life itself is a beautiful thing. As Mark Twain once said, "Age is mostly a matter of mind. If you don't mind, it doesn't matter." Where we get into trouble is the attempt to be something we are not, whether that's in our age or in our person. Such inner deception can also lead to self-defeat and depression.

We are the most appealing to others, and the happiest within, when we are completely ourselves. But it is a constant struggle because, as Scripture teaches, the world is always trying to press us into its mold. The mold of the world is the mold of the synthetic, the mold of the artificial, the mold of the celluloid —the "Plastic Person." The world cries, "You've got to be young and you've got to be tan. You've got to be thin and you've got to be rich. You've got to be great." But Scripture says, "You don't have to be any of those things. You simply have to be yourself—at any age— as God made you, available to Him so that He can work in and through you to bring about His kingdom and His glory. Now relax. Trust Him and be yourself!" It certainly isn't easy, but it *is* possible. American poet, writer, and artist E. E. Cummings once said:

> . . . to be nobody but yourself in a world which is doing its best, night and day, to make you everybody else,

means to fight the hardest battle which any human being can fight; and never stop fighting.[2]

So true! Sometimes it is tough to be me because I don't
like me. I'm disappointed in me. I'm embarrassed at
the way I look, or I'm not being understood and af-
firmed by somebody I want to love me. Clearly, without
doubt, there is nothing wrong with seeking to change
in ourselves what is able to be changed (I am a strong
advocate of that). But the essence of who we are—
our age, our sex, our looks, our past, our shortcomings,
our broken promises to ourselves, our unfulfilled
dreams—we must learn to live with and to accept for
what is. We must seek to walk in God's light and in
His counsel, realizing that contentment, acceptance,
love, compassion, vulnerability, and charm are the by-
products of an intimate relationship with Him, not the
results of conforming to the mandates and demands
of an insatiable world.

Growing older can be unbelievably exciting. It can
truly be a joyful experience as we look for new paths
of broadening our minds, enlarging our horizons, loving different people and new things, reaching across
prejudicial barriers. Simply put, it takes getting outside
ourselves and creating what is not, balanced and
blended with getting inside ourselves and accepting
what is.

In her book to which I made reference earlier, that
distinguished beauty, Sophia Loren, closes with these
encouraging words:

> So if you put on a little weight, find that you need glasses,
> get twinges of pain in your knees, and notice that a
> few dark brown spots are showing on your hands, don't
> despair. There is a fountain of youth: it is your mind,
> your talents, the creativity you bring to your life and

the lives of people you love. When you learn to tap this source, you will truly have defeated age.[3]

Let's do it. I know it will work. Then when the next birthday rolls around, we'll *really* have something to celebrate!

# 3
# Celebrating
# Mealtime

## BRINGING
## · HOME
## THE BACON

Having arrived at chapter 3, it is quite possible you
have the thought that Luci Swindoll promotes a philosophy which says, "To celebrate life, one must skip
around with a giddy grin on one's face, always encoun-
tering every situation with a smile (at worst) or an attitude of hilarity (at best)." I can understand how you
might think that, given the two chapters you've just
read—the ideas that happiness is for "now," don't wait
to celebrate, quit saving time but spend it for all its
worth, have a pinch of madness in your life, be creative,

accept yourself for the age you are, and find a distinct purpose there—all of that! Granted, I do believe there is a lot of truth to the adage, "A smile is better than a frown," but what I am trying to convey in this book, at its deepest level, is much more profound than that.

To fully enjoy life, to derive its greatest meaning and beauty, one needs to enter into it with not only the *look* of involvement and happiness, but the *spirit* of involvement, as well. Celebration is not just written on our faces, it must be living in our spirits. Therein lies a vast difference. When dedication to intentional involvement is true of our spirits, no matter our circumstances or our means, there will be no holding back from the richness life offers. Take a classic example: what can be more commonplace in our circumstances than mealtimes?

Generally, each of us eats two or three meals a day. No matter how large or small, we go through the everyday function of consuming food—somewhere, sometime, somehow—during each passing day. If we cut out this duty for long, we'd be victims of various health problems. Many of us, in fact, (myself included) have been known to add a fourth meal to our normal three. Sometimes, it doesn't stop there. On vacations there is often an overabundance of food, always available for the taking. This availability has gotten us into trouble, and that, too, can result in health problems. So understand at the outset I am not talking about excess in either direction. I'm talking about normal mealtimes—that time when we sit down with our family, business partners, friends, sweetheart, or by ourselves to plan, think, reflect, visit, laugh, chat, and lift each others' spirits while sharing food. Mealtime is fun time. It is an opportunity to feed our bodies and our souls. Quite often, mealtime is the highlight of the day.

Speaking of highlight, several years ago I decided I

would no longer use my real name when making restaurant reservations. If I used my name and couldn't keep the reservation for one reason or another, I found myself not wanting to call for another reservation at a later date for fear they would remember the name Swindoll and think, "Ah ha! Here's that flake who didn't show up when she was supposed to." Whereas, if I use a fictitious name and have to skip the reservation, who'll know the difference, or care? At least the Swindoll name will not be besmirched.

Since mealtime is often the highlight of my day, I started using Highlight as my restaurant reservation name. Generally speaking, my pals and mealtime partners are accustomed to it, but on occasion I forget to warn a new person who will be seated at my table. When I approach the maitre d' with, "Reservation for four please—Highlight," various business acquaintances often stare at me in disbelief as we are being escorted to our table. Explanations of my little game have served as both amusement and a unique icebreaker.

My friend Kurt taught me to begin this practice. The only difference is that he advised me to choose a fictitious name reflective of an occupation or station I always wanted to be but was not, such as "Parson," "Singer," "Monarch," "Pitcher," "Dancer," or "Sailor." I'll never forget the time Kurt and I walked into a restaurant where he had called for reservations (the first time he informed me of this stunt, *after* we were seated at our table), and announced, "Two, please . . . Star!" I giggled. So now, when Star and Highlight have the good fortune to dine together we have one great time of celebrating, whoever we may be! (There was also the time he was "Sorney Bandersnatch" and I was "Bernadette Petfarkin," but don't get me started.)

You will recall that in the introduction of this book

I referred to our poor, splendid souls and how they must fight for food. Mealtime for our bodies can be an ideal time to provide a bit of food for our souls, too—soul food! Even if you eat only one meal a day that is an occasion to relax, come apart from the routine and give your soul an unexpected perk. Soul nourishment reveals itself in numerous ways throughout our daily lives. There is a measure of contentment that is characteristic of a soul which has been fed. And it is quite enjoyable to be with those who demonstrate that contentment, is it not? The following is a list of soul food suggestions to try during mealtimes. They are only suggestions. Be creative. Put on your thinking cap and come up with some ideas of your own to make mealtime more of a celebration, with others or by yourself.

*Mealtime with others:*

- From the moment you are seated at the table until you get up to leave, everything verbalized must be spoken either in rhyme or sung. If you discuss an issue, it must be done in poetry or rendered in song. The same is true of asking for some item to be passed. Example: "Pass the butter to me mutter before you pass it to me brutter."

- If you are with only one other person, each of you choose a topic of interest you've never discussed before. Do a bit of research on it prior to arriving at the table and have an SYI party (share your ignorance). You'll learn something new—count on it.

- Try conversing in another language, or if one of your kids is taking another language in school, have him or her teach you five new words of that language and use them at the table. You'll be feeding your mind as well as your soul and body! I have a friend who lived in Italy for over a year after her college graduation. She now speaks fluent Italian. In fact, I took a few Italian lessons from her during the days I sang with the Dallas Civic Opera Chorus. When she and I are able to get together for a meal, I'll occasionally say, "Hey Judy, let's speak only in Italian." I don't talk as much as usual during those meals, but I do muddle along and it's fun. She spends a lot of time helping me, but she doesn't seem to mind. It keeps her in practice, too.

- Go out on a limb and cook everything in the center-fold of *Gourmet* for any given month. Decorate the table. Use your best dishes. Light the candles. Turn off the television.
- Let your kids plan, cook, and serve the meal (no matter how messy the kitchen becomes). You make the place cards, clean up the mess, and do the dishes.
- Go on a breakfast picnic and listen to the sounds around you. Look for things that are beautiful, unique, or fleeting. Enjoy it and talk about it to-gether.
- Don't open any cans. Don't incorporate anything in the meal with the word "instant" on the box. Using only fresh ingredients, prepare a meal you've never had before and invite over at least two people you love but have never entertained in your home. Be daring!

*Mealtime alone:*

- Go to an expensive restaurant. Don't take a book or magazine to read. Order at least three courses and take a long time eating, savoring the taste of each one. Eavesdrop on conversations around you. Think about your own life in relation to the people you hear talking.
- Have breakfast in bed: you'll have to get up to make it, but that's all right. Use the good dishes. Once

that's done, put everything on a tray and take it back to bed with the morning newspaper. Don't hurry. Pamper yourself.

- Throughout your meal, talk to God. Out loud. Thank Him for your food, your health, your appetite to enjoy it. Sing a song or two of praise (not with your mouth full, please!). When you're through eating, ask God to provide an angel to do the dishes—then get up and do them, knowing He has! Have some fun with the Lord. Thank Him for the joy of laughter.

- Pack a picnic for one. Make either the biggest salad (with at least seven ingredients) or the fattest sandwich you've ever eaten in your life. Put everything in it you can think of. Carry a small thermos of coffee or tea with your entree in a back pack and go on a two-mile hike. Your reward for hiking, while you sit under a shade tree, is that fabulous meal. When you get home allow yourself one Godiva chocolate or a Snickers candy bar or your favorite dessert. After all this—finishing your hike, meal, dessert—sing the Doxology and rejoice in the delight of simply being alive.

- Eat in your living room by candlelight, listening to your favorite record album.

- During your meal, think about your best friend or sweetheart—what he or she means to you and why. Compose a letter to that individual in your head. After you've finished eating, write the letter, stamp it, and mail it that day.

- Bake your favorite muffins. Use food coloring and dye some red, others blue, leaving a few plain. As you enjoy two or three with a cup of your favorite beverage, read *The Declaration of Independence* and be glad you live in America. If you own one, fly the American flag. Remind yourself that were it not for your forefathers you wouldn't be sitting there enjoying red, white, and blue muffins and tea: Savor your independence. You're not lonely— you're independent. There are dozens of perks to being independent.

Two of my favorite dining out places to celebrate mealtimes may come as a surprise to you. My reason for frequenting either place is because of the people it attracts; the mealtime becomes a study in human nature, not just a dining experience. One is a public counter, the other a truck stop. In some ways, each of these eating establishments encourages a culture all its own—the latter more than the former, perhaps— but each place seems to thrive on a certain "type," unique unto itself but different from the other. I love to go to these "hangouts" because I love to observe people.

The public counters—those great formica scallops flanked by simulated leather stools found from coast to coast—seem to draw individuals who are always "on their way," in a hurry, or on the move. Some are on their way up the ladder of success with little or no time for leisurely dining, so the counter offers speed and decisiveness; no dawdling. Others are on their way into or out of a meaningful relationship. In this case, the counter gives that person a semi-private place to fantasize or brood, whichever the desire may be. The third typical counter-sitters are on their way to a meeting, a rendezvous, a ball game, a shopping spree. The counter provides these people with a place for a quick bite or a fast cup of coffee.

During my sojourns at counter-hopping through life I have rarely engaged anyone in conversation. Between counter neighbors there is little conviviality or exchange of words. Because I expect this, I usually take a book, magazine, or newspaper to peruse during my meal until someone interesting looking comes in, in which case my attention turns to their demeanor. The best example took place one morning at a Big Boy restaurant counter, not five minutes from my apartment. I had run up there one Saturday for breakfast to grab an English muffin and coffee prior to going into Los Angeles to shop. Morning newspaper in hand, I took the only counter seat left, next to a young man who was about halfway through his meal. We said nothing. After ordering, I opened the paper to scan the front page when I noticed out of the corner of my eye he kept looking in my direction as if eager to talk, occasionally drumming his fingers on the counter. Finally, while still seated, he took money from his pocket to pay for his meal and, looking straight at me, blurted:

"My wife just had a baby."

"Oh . . . how exciting. A boy or a girl?"

"A little girl."

"That's great. How can you just sit there so calmly? Why aren't you running up and down the street passing out cigars or something?"

"Well," he said, smilingly, "this isn't my first. She's our third girl. We have three girls now."

"And I guess you wanted a boy, huh?"

"Oh, well, yes. But, you know—I'm glad she's here and healthy, and that's what's important."

"That's right."

"The only problem is that we can't agree on a name for her. My wife wants to name her Lucy, but I don't know. I don't much like the name 'Lucy.' "

"Oh really? Why? I think it's a nice name."

"It sounds average . . . and, every Lucy I've ever known was big and fat. I guess I think when she grows up she'll be fat."

"Not necessarily."

"You know what I mean, you just have this preconceived notion. What do you think is a good name for a girl? What's your name?"

"Luci."

"Oh gosh, I'm sorry," he said, turning red and trying to smile. "Uh . . . can I buy you a cup of coffee?"

"How 'bout a hot fudge sundae?"

Truck stop mealtimers, on the other hand, are vastly different from counter sitters. They are a breed set apart from the life around them—clannish, specialists, loners. I became interested in truck stop culture when I was a college student and traveled between my college town and hometown with some degree of frequency. There was a heavily visited local truck stop known as Polly's on that stretch of road, and I usually stopped there because the food was good, the service was fast, and the truckers were fascinating. Besides, a sign hanging over the kitchen door always amused me: "Our cow died so we don't need your bull." Truckers don't mince words.

These energetic men and their waitresses speak the same language. They talk about the food, their trucks, their families, love affairs, dances, murders. No dull stuff around here. Over the long hauls and down unrolling highways they cover the surface of the nation, eating mountains of food and drinking oceans of coffee.

Now that I am many years and miles removed from Polly's, I have discovered a new truck stop I frequent whenever possible. It's north of Los Angeles on the everbusy I-5 just south of Bakersfield. A colossal conglomerate of shops, rest area, and service station, it also encompasses a large eating facility named Country Pride. Isn't that a great name? Not long ago, I stopped there for breakfast. Spotting "biscuits and sausage gravy" on the menu I was immediately reminded of Polly's, and I ordered it. It was a huge meal, served in a platter! I should be grateful it wasn't transferred from kitchen to table in a wheelbarrow. I could hardly walk afterwards. Maybe that guy was right about fat Lucys.

Were I called upon to designate my preferred meal, however, I would have to say it would be a gourmet picnic, such as something I would pack and take to the Hollywood Bowl, or perhaps French cuisine. Both I love with a passion!

I am a dedicated picnicker. A few years ago when I was on a short vacation in Vail, Colorado, a friend gave me a recipe book she bought there which I have used and enjoyed repeatedly, *The Picnic Gourmet*. It is a superb volume of marvelous, tasty recipes for every type of picnic imaginable, and suggestions to entice you to indulge your picnic urge as often as possible. As one of the co-authors, Connie Maricich, says, "Picnicking is the highest form of human entertainment." Agreed. It's an extraordinary opportunity to celebrate being alive. I have picnicked since childhood with my family and friends, both here in America and abroad, on land and sea, in the mountains, in the desert, and in moving vehicles. These occasions are definitely among my most pleasant memories.

As far as French cuisine is concerned, there is no denying my first love: the famous Ma Maison restaurant in Los Angeles. Just knowing I have an upcoming reservation there produces an unparalleled *joie de vivre* in my spirit. It has the most delicious food in the world. Find out for yourself. Go there sometime and order *saumon ou bar en croûte* (salmon in puff pastry). It's served in the shape of a fish, complete with head, eyes, body, and tail—a highlight without comparison!

Unfortunately, eating at Ma Maison can only be enjoyed on very special occasions. The meal is too rich for one's blood and billfold on a daily basis. I save up and make plans and wait my turn. Then, when the time comes to begin the meal, I die a thousand deaths from sheer joy. What a way to go!

It's a peculiar thing, but the first "big" meal I ever cooked was French cuisine, served at 9:30 P.M., on December 11, 1961 (one of my most enjoyable memories of celebrating mealtime).

About a month earlier, I had bought a copy of the famous *Brennan's New Orleans Cookbook,* newly published that year, and a pound of Canadian bacon, purchased through a mail order catalogue—one of those packaged foods you buy wondering how or when you'll eat it, but you get it anyway because it's Christmas. From time to time I picked up my new recipe book for casual reading, remembering how delicious the food was at the original Brennan's in New Orleans, where I had eaten some years before. I drooled with every page.

Knowing my friend Charlotte was having a birthday in December, I thought one day while drooling, "Why not have a late-night breakfast? That would be loads of fun—and different. I'll cook two or three recipes from this Brennan's book and surprise everybody with my culinary abilities, including myself. Even if the meal is awful we'll have a few laughs and a fun celebration. If it's good, . . . who knows? Maybe I'll open a restaurant."

After those thoughts I began looking at the recipe book with a different eye. No longer was this an exercise in casual reading, this became my obsession. All I could think about was that dinner party. I designed and made invitations—all individually handpainted with the famous, colorful Brennan's rooster on front.

Inside I listed time, date, place, and purpose. The friends I invited all offered to help in any way they could, partly out of self-defense since they were aware I was a novice at cooking, and partly because they immediately got into the spirit of the party. Each of us counted the days until "The Breakfast."

I was operating under a handicap—I had never cooked anything of this magnitude or quality before, nor anything French, so I had fear and trembling in my bones. But, in keeping with my philosophy, I kept thinking, "Luci, there's no time like the present. What have you got to lose but a little money, a night of work, and nine friends? Go for it . . . it'll be fun. Anybody can take Charlotte to a French restaurant. You be different. Prepare a spectacular meal in your own home." Like a fool, I ploughed ahead.

Have you ever tried your hand at French cuisine? Then you'll know what I mean when I say there's *lots* of preparation involved—the sauces alone!! After beginning the meal with Grilled Grapefruit which was simple enough (and delicious) I chose a dish entitled "Eggs Hussarde," calling for two exotic sauces. One reason I made the selection of that particular egg recipe for my entree was because the sauce recipes were printed on facing pages, thereby permitting me to look at them simultaneously. I don't think I've *ever* worked so hard in the kitchen before. In the first place, I have never chopped so much in my life. My previous culinary talents consisted of little more than boiling an egg or two. Would this never end? After chopping there was simmering, stirring, watching, waiting, and what the Bible calls "seasoned prayer."

It was unforgettable. A crisp chill of late fall was in the evening air, everything was decorated for Christmas, everybody was in a festive mood, and the most heavenly aromatic smells engulfed each guest at the opening of the front door. Delicious smells. Inviting smells. Those unmistakable aromas that make one breathe deeply and say, "Good grief, what *is* that?" while marching straight to the kitchen.

Finally, the time came to put everything together. With the continual help of my friend Martha, a real gourmet cook whom I nicknamed "Chop-Chop," we got the entree on each plate, decorated each with a small sprig of parsley, and carried the presentation to the table. *Vóila!* I must admit, with the first bite, in unison we yelled. Truly, it was delicious in spite of my naïveté. My risk had paid off and the time, energy, and money was worth every ounce of the investment. Charlotte kept saying, "I never had such a delicious meal for my birthday. This is great." But the best was yet to come.

For dessert I wanted to create something flaming— couldn't be French and not flame. "Eclair Eugene" was my choice. There was a line in the recipe which read, "Just as flame dies, spoon sauce (another sauce!) over eclair filled with ice cream." I thought flame would never die. It grew in intensity, causing the chocolate to get hotter and hotter, ultimately making it splatter—on the table, on the wall, on the guests, and all over the pages of my open recipe book.

With the first mouthful there were more cries of ecstacy. Everyone laughed and yelled and carried on in abandonment, just as people should during a time of celebration. The last line of the dessert recipe read "one serving," which proved to be a disappointment to us. We all came back for more, but I simply ran out of ingredients . . . not to mention flame, energy, and chopping time. We all had as terrific a time as the birthday girl herself!

Keep in mind the key to enjoying mealtime is in the spirit, not necessarily in the food. Celebrating a meal doesn't have to be for a birthday or an anniversary. Neither does it have to be for Thanksgiving or Christmas. It can be today. Any day. Every day. At home, at a counter, on a picnic, at a truck stop, or in a fancy French restaurant. It doesn't matter. The spirit of fun and enjoyment is what matters. So . . . bring home the bacon and find new ways to enjoy it.

Wolfgang Puck writes:

Cooking is my "kinderspeil"—my child's play. You can make it yours, too. And while you're cooking, don't forget to share and laugh. Laugh a great deal, and with much love—it enhances the flavor of food.[1]

He should know. He's the chef at Ma Maison.

# 4
# Celebrating

# Camaraderie

## ENJOYING
## THE
## FELLOWSHIP

A poet once described friends as "the sunshine of life." I myself have found that the day is certainly much brighter when I'm sharing it with my friends. Enjoying fellowship is one of life's sweetest blessings and joys. What would we do without people and the many shadings of companionship and camaraderie? We need friends in our lives, friends with whom we not only discuss "deep" issues and confide our secrets, fears, or sorrows, but with whom we can laugh, play, and even cry. The best times in life are made a thousand times better when shared with a dear friend.

Camaraderie is definitely a part of friendship, and camaraderie itself can often produce friendships, too. When we reach out to others, they reach out to us. It's a two-way street, a street practically lined with balloons and streamers in celebration of the unique bonds of friendship.

Not long ago I was fortunate enough to have been invited as a speaker for a "conference afloat," a seminar cruise sponsored by my brother Chuck's radio ministry. The Insight for Living staff had chosen the theme "Experience the Fellowship" for the weeklong cruise. No other motto could have depicted the camaraderie any better!

For seven fun-filled days, the twelve hundred of us on board the ship spent every moment enjoying the entertainment, worship, fun, food, new friendships, and the breathtaking sights of the Caribbean islands. I can't imagine a better setting for celebrating camaraderie! We had at our disposal dozens of on-board shops, lounges, a movie theater, a huge library, a television station, a game room, three swimming pools, a huge sundeck, and even an ice cream parlor. Sheer luxury. The islands provided plenty of white sandy beaches lined with umbrellas, swaying palm trees, wonderful calypso bands serenading us with island melodies, and beautiful turquoise water teeming with a kaleidoscope of fish and sealife. Insight for Living held daily Bible lessons on the life of Moses, offered early morning aerobic classes for those of us who had taken advantage of the ship's seven daily meals, sponsored activities for teenagers, singles, and adult groups, and gathered us all together for lots of music and song. All needs and desires were met for the body, soul, and spirit. But the best and most memorable part of the whole week was the camaraderie.

Every day I followed the Insight motto and experienced the fellowship. Among old friends, among new acquaintances, the theme of the cruise continually manifested itself. My favorite times were at Table 151, where I had been assigned for mealtimes. The eight of us became fast friends almost upon our first encounter. And together, we proved to be a notorious collection of funsters, punsters, pranksters, and gangsters in a mild but off-the-wall sense. Each mealtime was spiced with craziness, frivolity, harebrained chatter, wild "but true" stories, recounting of various escapades, spilling of embarrassing confessions, telling of jokes, spinning of fantasies, gales of laughter, plenty of high jinks and picture taking, and general nuttiness.

The last night of the cruise, in addition to the three already planned festivities, Table 151 decided to have its own farewell celebration. We had drawn names for gift-giving, and that evening we presented each other with zany limericks, songs, and ditties, along with such presents as a homemade collage of the cruise, poems, relics from the islands, and I even got a live hermit crab (which I mistook for a tarantula). We were the object of a few stares and raised eyebrows, but I cannot remember having so much fun. No doubt about it. Friends are *indeed* "the sunshine of life."

Companionship also reflects the value of our own selves. Gail Sheehy, the author of two phenomenal bestsellers, *Passages* and *Pathfinders,* puts it this way:

> By listening, by caring, by playing you back to yourself, friends ratify your better instincts and endorse your unique worth. Friends validate you.[1]

Do you know what camaraderie does for me at its most basic level? It serves as a kind of therapy, because there are no demands involved. It programs itself into the memory disks of my mind and heart so that on gloomy days, when I'm alone, I can play back all those good times of fellowship stored there.

Another credit for companions and comrades is that they are not (necessarily) our marriage partners; therefore, there is no feeling of sexual possessiveness. Comrades in fellowship are easily shared. There is no dominance or dependence. No judgments. No requirements. No unfulfilled expectations. There is only great relaxation, which is wonderful. Camaraderie is born out of the context of conviviality and nourished on sociability. But it requires a little effort. One cannot experience nor enjoy camaraderie while remaining antisocial. It just won't happen.

Camaraderie is therapeutic, without demands, and it thrives on sociability. In addition, it often produces or reveals a rich by-product: affinity, that spontaneous attraction to each other. That was certainly the case at our cruise table, wasn't it? We each enjoyed music, theater, words, antics, playfulness, food, fun, and our mutual and individual love for the Lord. And even though our tastes and personalities varied, we fit together perfectly as the best of friends. Around Table 151 each day of the cruise we felt "at home." From time to time I couldn't help but be reminded of those lines from Hermann Hesse's novel, *Demian:*

> One never reaches home, but where paths that have affinity for each other intersect, the whole world looks like home for a time.

At that table, in our camaraderie, the whole world looked like home.

As I've already pointed out, camaraderie thrives on sociability. But what if you are among those individuals who rarely feel "at home" . . . what if you don't know how to open a conversation with a stranger? You're afraid to begin. What then? This is an issue which people often ask me about—"How do I learn to reach out?" The first thing I'd say to you is "Take heart." There are thousands of people out there just like you. Even though you may feel like the only one in the boat, you're not. And the good news is that you don't have to stay there. You *can* learn to reach out.

There are numerous places and situations in which you can reach out to establish friendships. First of all, however, you must make a mental pledge to yourself that you will change your entire line of thinking when it comes to overcoming the shyness or fear that leads to antisocial behavior. Tell yourself that you *are* a fun person to be around, that you *do* have important opinions and ideas, that you *can* be spontaneous and witty and charming. And then go out there and start practicing your new attitude toward life by meeting new people.

- Sign up for a class on one of your major interests, be it art, music, photography, literature, electronics, or a new language. Get to know the other students seated around you, and volunteer your home for a practice or study session.

- Become involved in your church's ministry to those in your age group. The church is an excellent source of providing new friends for everyone from school-aged children to college students, from singles to young marrieds to senior citizens. Most groups also plan special outings to let people get to know each other even better.

- Join a health club. Not only will you meet lots of people, you'll also feel great and look great. Besides, working out in the weight room and relaxing in

the sauna are great ice-breaking topics in themselves.

• Volunteer one day a month to work with patients
in a nursing home, with a charitable organization,
or with underprivileged children. The rewards are
just as great as the people you'll meet.

• Plan your vacation around a specific goal-oriented
tour, such as the Insight for Living cruise to the
Caribbean. There are hundreds of archaelogical ex-
peditions to Israel, getaway packages for Christian
single adults, and short-term mission adventures
throughout the United States and in practically every foreign country. You can even volunteer to be
a chaperone for high school students traveling Europe in the summer.

One of the most helpful books I have ever read on
developing friendships is by the famous ABC inter-
viewer, Barbara Walters. In her book, *How to Talk
with Practically Anybody about Practically Anything,*
she offers guidelines, tips, and her own humorously
candid stories on improving social conversation. Although I love to visit with people and was already putting many of her ideas into practice, I learned new
pointers which I have since applied, resulting in richer
and more enjoyable dialogue with people. You'll *love*
the book. Get a copy today. Begin reading it tonight.
Start applying it tomorrow. In one of her suggestions
toward improving conversation, Ms. Walters writes:

> . . . the most consistently endearing human trait is
> warmth. *Everybody* responds to the person who radiates
> friendliness from a serene core. Such people are lovely
> to be around because they don't reject or belittle and,
> best of all, they bring out the best, most generous quali-
> ties in the people they encounter, and make them feel
> marvelous about themselves.[2]

Aside from an occasional hermit or two, most of us would like to indulge in a lot of camaraderie. But, as Barbara Walters pointed out, it takes some time and energy to develop the friendships necessary for such fellowship. Without contributing a little effort of our own, we can hardly expect everyone to immediately and automatically like us. Think back to some of the people you deemed as "popular." Remember that cheerleader in high school who always said "Hi" to everyone she passed in the hall? Remember the neighbors who were always inviting you over for grilled burgers or left a standing invitation to babysit your kids? Remember that guy at the office who always asked how you were doing, sincerely expecting an answer? Remember your roommate in college who was always coming up with spontaneous suggestions like the late-night swim party or driving to the lake to study for finals?

Barbara Walters says a lot in her book about the importance of warmth, honesty, compassion, charm, kindness, genuine interest, listening, gratitude, wit, spontaneity, and the other characteristics we all want to possess in the fine art of creating and enjoying fellowship. She touches the real key to the secret of camaraderie—making others feel good about themselves.

You don't have to go on a Caribbean cruise to celebrate camaraderie. Have fun where you are! There is a lot you can do to enjoy the fellowship of old or new friends:

- Hold an old-fashioned pot-luck supper in your back yard or a nearby park. Invite everyone you can think of, and plan for a sunny day.

- Instigate a daily mid-morning coffee break for your departmental co-workers. You'll discuss more than business, I guarantee it.

- Take several friends window-shopping for clothes, cars, jewelry, or furniture, and go out for pizza afterward to celebrate all the money you saved by not buying anything.

- Spend the day with friends at a nearby amusement park, zoo, pool, or beach.

- Make or buy some colorful kites for you and your friends to fly on a bright and windy day. You'll make even more friends as people come over to watch.

- Throw a party to celebrate a raise, a promotion, a great report card, Groundhog's Day, the victory of a favorite ball team, your state's independence day, the beginning of spring, or Barbra Streisand's birthday.

- Get together with friends for an early evening walk or jog every day. Not only will you enjoy the camaraderie, you'll also appreciate the benefits when it comes time to try on your swimsuit.

- Go roller skating, skiing, biking, or hiking one afternoon. You'll enjoy laughing at and with each other.

- Make it a point to try to be more understanding each day, to listen more, to be more open, to express genuine interest, to be open to more spontaneity, and to get more involved. Try saying "yes" more often than "no."

As a final tribute to the camaraderie of Table 151, I must close with an account of something that occurred the very morning we disembarked from our week of fun and frolic. Picture, if you will, everyone from the Insight for Living Conference sitting around in one of the ship's larger lounges, awaiting an announcement over the loudspeaker that the ship had passed customs and its passengers could leave. The eight of us were sitting together one last time—continuing our marathon conversations and laughter, when suddenly, over the speaker system came this unexpected disclosure: "Will Luci Swindoll of Cabin B188 please come to the purser's office and pay her bar bill?" I could have died. Naturally, the whole place exploded into yells, jeers, finger pointing, and laughter. Here I was, one of Insight for Living's guest speakers for twelve hundred Christians, ignoring an outstanding bar bill. No matter the fact that it was for two Diet Pepsis I had signed for the first day of the cruise, which I had forgotten about—and that was *before* we changed cabins. I guess the "outstanding bar bill" is one thing I'll never live down.

We ended the cruise with hugs and tears and more laughter, promising to rendezvous again. My outrageous table companions and I had formed an unusually strong bond of friendship in seven short days, a bond strengthened and enhanced by our kinship as children of God.

With comrades like that, how can you help *but* celebrate?

# 5
# Celebrating Reunions

## REMEMBERING WITH NOSTALGIA

At the base of the Statue of Liberty is inscribed the greatest "Welcome Home" message that has probably ever been written:

> Give me your tired, your poor,
> Your huddled masses yearning to breathe free,
> The wretched refuse of your teeming shore,
> Send these, the homeless, tempest-tossed to me:
> I lift my lamp beside the golden door.[1]

Isn't that a wonderful invitation for the weary-worn traveler to come home to rest? It expresses the spirit

of that great sculptured symbol which first greets those
who arrive on the shores of America.

Those words were set to music by Irving Berlin for
his show, *Miss Liberty*, and I sang a choral arrangement
of it in college. I could hardly get through it each time
without crying because I was so moved by the meaning
it conveyed. It made me feel enveloped by loving, gi-
gantic hands, assuring me of peace, protection, and
warmth—like the hands we see nowadays in some television commercials for insurance. If they could talk
they would say, "Crawl in here and you'll be okay.
I'll take care of you."

Singer/songwriter Kenny Loggins describes a homecoming as being "celebrated home," one where friends
"turn on every love light in the place." Isn't that won-
derfully descriptive of a perfect reunion? I think it's
a fabulous idea.

Next time you're expecting the return of a loved
one, celebrate the reunion. Go out of your way to make
it unforgettable. Turn on every love light in the place
and surround that person with the circle of friends
they've been missing. Then, later, when they are all
alone, apart from those they love, they will remember
it all with nostalgia. No doubt about it.

I cannot tell you the number of times I have been
celebrated home exactly like that. Located in Sebasto-
pol, California, just north of San Francisco, is "Rainbow's End," the charming home of two of my dearest
friends. They named it "Rainbow's End" because, to
them, it is just that: the pot of gold at the end of the
rainbow. I can't say that I blame them! It's beautiful.
It sits in the midst of hills and valleys, meadows and
wildflowers, a running stream, and huge trees. I go
there three or four times a year, dragging my weary
body and frazzled mind in search of solace and tran-
quillity. Never am I disappointed.

And do they ever know how to plan a reunion! This weary-worn traveler always feels at home and at peace. When I walk through the door I am greeted with the smell of fudge coming from the kitchen, vases of flowers from the yard, fresh vegetables from their own garden, my preferred choice of music from their stereo, and every love light in the place turned on! I am truly celebrated home and it's fantastic. But that moment of homecoming is only the beginning.

During my visits there, I have a bedroom and bath exclusively my own. No trespassing! Right off the bat it's like a lovely hotel where I don't pay the bill—privacy, security, comfort, and room service. They wait on me hand and foot. They cook gourmet meals, provide fresh ground coffee any time of the day or night, and encourage me to rest, relax, and do nothing. So, in my mandated state of inertia and torpidity I become like a hibernating animal settling into a long winter's nap, or I mosey around the house doing all sorts of fun things to feed my soul:

- I pull volumes from the shelves of my friends' massive library and re-read favorite passages I had forgotten were there. I muse on various lines of poetry. I choose the book I want to take to bed with me that night to have drop on my nose while falling asleep.

- I select the stack of records which I know we most enjoy and want to hear and play them in any order I like.

- I take long walks or lounge on the sundeck or fly a kite or watch hot air balloons drift over the valley.

- I sit in front of the fire and listen to the rain.

- I visit endlessly and laugh heartily with my fascinating companions.

- I reflect with them upon our twenty years of yesterdays together—the playful and enchanting escapades of our more energetic and abandoned youths.
- I design, bake, and decorate a homemade chocolate cake for dessert, after the dinner they are preparing.
- I play with the animals—a dog and four cats.
- I feed the chickens.
- I gather flowers and arrange them in vases.
- I decide the menu for the day.
- I pick apples and pears from their trees, vegetables from their garden, and blackberries from their berry patch up the road.
- I drive the pickup truck (watch out world!).
- I write in the Guest Book.
- I take pictures.
- I type a friendly letter or two . . . "Wish you were here, you wouldn't believe. . . ."
- I reminisce upon the numerous occasions we have shared and the times my dear friends have celebrated me home at "Rainbow's End."

No matter how little or how much time I can spend at their house, I try very hard to live in the present moment. I don't want to think about saying "goodbye." I hate goodbyes. They make me sad and quiet and often put me in a bad mood. Even though I know the old adage, "Love knows not its own depth until the hour of separation," I'm in favor of finding some other way to know the depth of love.

I like reunions, not partings. I read once that "the pain of parting is nothing to the joy of meeting again." I can't agree that the pain is "nothing," but I know from experience that the celebration of meeting again generally outweighs the sorrow and memory of saying goodbye.

The ideal illustration of a celebrated reunion, probably the best representation in the history of humanity, is that of the return of the Prodigal Son. Talk about "wretched refuse" in singular form—this was it! Woven within this tragic event, however, is the perfect exemplification of how to make somebody know you have welcomed them home with nothing held back. Let's analyze the story for a few minutes.

Jesus is telling it in the form of a parable in Luke 15:11–32. Briefly put, there was a father who had two sons. The younger son decided to leave home and asked his father for the share of inheritance money that would one day belong to him. The father divided the money between the two sons and the younger took his and left, going far away into another country. He wasted his money in riotous living until finally he had absolutely nothing left. When a famine came to the land, he was forced to go to work. Soliciting employment from one of the local citizens in the area, he was given a job and sent into the fields to feed pigs. There, in the pigpen, in utter mental and material destitution, he came to his senses. He realized he had acted impetuously and foolishly and determined he'd go back home, confess his remorse to his dad, and offer to be his hired servant since he felt he was no longer worthy to be called a son.

At this point, I want to pick up the story from Scripture because it so perfectly conveys what I'm trying to say about celebrating a reunion. I'll begin at Luke 15:20, as taken from *The Living Bible:*

> So he returned home to his father. And while he was still a long distance away, his father saw him coming, and was filled with loving pity and ran and embraced him and kissed him.
>
> His son said to him, "Father, I have sinned against heaven and you, and am not worthy of being called your son—"

But the father said to the slaves, "Quick! Bring the finest robe in the house and put it on him. And a jeweled ring for his finger; and shoes! And kill the calf we have in the fattening pen. We must celebrate with a feast, for this son of mine was dead and has returned to life. He was lost and is found." So the party began.

Stop there for a minute. Without getting into the deep theological ramifications of this passage, let me point out a couple of important aspects of celebrating someone home. Those aspects come up so clearly in the above-referenced verses.

First of all, when people are reunited, I believe there should be an open demonstration of affection if that is in keeping with their natures. Oftentimes, we hold back in embarrassment for fear of what people around us will think. Don't be embarrassed! Go ahead and hug each other. Kiss each other if that's the way you both feel upon meeting. Warmly welcome the person you've missed.

One reason I love to go to airports is that I enjoy watching the display of emotions between people as they are reunited. Haven't you been waiting for a plane to arrive, bringing home someone you love and are eager to see, when beside you there steps up a guy holding a bouquet of flowers or a box of candy (sometimes both!). You immediately think, "Wow! I can't wait to get a look at who's going to get off this plane to meet *him*. Probably his sweetheart . . . I gotta see this!" So, even if your party arrives first, you stick around to witness a starry-eyed, willowy young woman disembark and fall into the waiting arms of her Prince Charming. Everybody loves a lover.

Affection should not be saved, then shared only between lovers, however. That's ridiculous. Everybody appreciates affection and a warm display of greeting. Okay, maybe not *everybody*, but certainly the majority. Reach out! Embrace! Women with women, men with men, friends, family members, young, old, different races, different colors. Don't be afraid to genuinely celebrate those first moments of reunion with demonstrative affection. It breaks down all sorts of barriers. Note in our Scripture passage that when the son started confessing his sorrow and his remorse to his dad, "I am not good enough to be called a son," the father ignored that completely. Never referred to it. He was thinking, "My son is home!!! Let me kiss him. Let me hold him. Let's celebrate!"

I read in the newspaper recently of a comment made by a friend of one of the Americans held hostage for seventeen days in Lebanon, prior to their release. The friend said, "I can't wait till my buddy comes home. I'm going to give him the world's biggest bear hug and never let him go." That's the kind of demonstration I mean—a true feeling of love and joy in reunion.

Letting somebody know you're glad to see them is nothing to be ashamed of nor something only to be expressed in private. You're not going to be labeled, and if you are, so what? That's the "labeler's" problem, not yours. Leo Buscaglia once said, "A loving individual frees himself from labels." Labels are words, and we cannot allow labels *or* words to dictate our actions. "You, if you are a loving person, will rule words and not allow them to rule you," continues Buscaglia. "You will tell yourself what this word means only after you find out by experience what it means; not by believing what people have told you it means." Good point. *Very* good point! If you feel like being warm and demonstrative, do it, and don't be afraid of what those standing around will think. Chances are they'll wish they had someone to welcome them in the same way. Reunions imply affection in its warmest sense. Feel free to give it.

Second, note that the items the father called for from

the servant were the very best: the clothes, the ring, the shoes, the calf. The reunion principle is that when you celebrate a homecoming, you are to use your *finest*. Don't save things for a "better day;" this *is* that better day. Remember from chapter 1 the story of the young woman who had died unexpectedly while saving all her best for that "special occasion" which never seemed to come? A reunion between loved ones is of *all* times as special as it can get, so use the best you have—everything you can think of!

Several years ago, some friends and I took a long-awaited and long-saved-for trip to northern Italy to visit my chorus master and his wife. They were Italians who came to America every fall and worked with us in the Dallas Civic Opera. Their home was tucked away in a picturesque village called Barbania Canavese which was nestled in the foothills of the Italian Alps, a hamlet so small that it wasn't even on the map. But beautiful?! Oh! We had not seen Maestro and Signora Mola in months and had *never* been to their home. We were out of our minds with excitement. It was early spring and fruit trees were in bloom everywhere with an intoxicating aroma filling the air. We tooled along those mountain roads in a little Fiat, singing and talking and laughing at the top of our lungs. When we finally arrived at their home, it literally took our breath away. As if the reunion itself were not enough for our souls, there was all this beauty in their dwelling and the surrounding scenery. Too much!

Their mountain home, with its mixture of Italian and Swiss decor, was without doubt one of the most interesting places I have ever had the good fortune to visit. It was *full* of pleasing and artistic objects which reflected their years of marriage, travel, collecting, working with the opera, and the love of their friends and family. They had beautiful relics and photographs from dozens of "greats" who are famous in musical and artistic circles the world over.

But what really struck me more than anything else was that when we sat down to dinner that evening around a huge, handcarved table laden with much food and drink, Signora Mola served meat from a fatted calf they had actually raised, and had butchered in honor of our visit. I sat at the table and cried because I felt so loved and privileged. It was a wonderful moment. I thought of the Prodigal Son. Even though I was not returning from years of wild and profligate living into the arms of my forgiving father, I was returning from months of separation from my loving friends. They had greeted us with warm affection. They had used their very best. They had even killed and served the fatted calf! It was unforgettable.

Now, let's pick up our Scripture account of the Prodigal Son to get two other ingredients for celebrating a reunion. Beginning at verse 25:

> Meanwhile, the older son was in the fields working; when he returned home, he heard dance music coming from the house, and he asked one of the servants what was going on.
>
> "Your brother is back," he was told, "and your father has killed the calf we were fattening and has prepared a great feast to celebrate his coming home again unharmed."
>
> The older brother was angry and wouldn't go in. His father came out and begged him, but he replied, "All these years I've worked hard for you and never once refused to do a single thing you told me to; and in all that time you never gave me even one young goat for a feast with my friends. Yet when this son of yours comes back after spending your money on prostitutes, you celebrate by killing the finest calf we have on the place."

"Look, dear son," his father said to him, "you and I are very close, and everything I have is yours. But it is right to celebrate. For he is your brother; and he was dead and has come back to life! He was lost and is found!"

The third component is a very real and vital part of celebrating reunions—music. "As he came closer to the house he heard the sound of music and dancing." It is impossible for me to say enough about music— its magic, its ability to unlock our hearts, its profound affect upon who we are and how we feel. In every culture and civilization that has tread upon this earth, the sounds of music have been at its very heart. The rejoicing father and the Prodigal Son *had* to sing and dance. They simply could not contain themselves. They needed neither rehearsal nor audience. They had a freelance, unscheduled performance for each other. For joy. For God. All they needed to make music were happy hearts—and they had those.

I can hardly recall a homecoming in my life where music was not a fundamental part. The night we spent with the Molas was characterized by music. After our celebration feast around the table, I recall our going into the music room where Maestro Mola sat down at his enormous black Steinway and played as my friend Bianca sang arias from four or five different operas. Without accompaniment, I sang Negro spirituals (which all Italians *love* because of their simple, poignant words and melodies). Maestro played Chopin sonatas and even as the rest of us were reluctantly heading off to bed, he was putting records on the stereo for our enjoyment. A barely audible Bruch's "Violin Concerto No. 1" lulled us to sleep that night (and has since become one of my absolute favorites). Isn't it strange? I don't remember what we talked about after dinner that night but I do recall every bit of the music.

When I was a child and my family visited my grandparents in another city on holidays or special occasions, there was almost constant music in the house. We had piano music or guitar music or singing all the time, and sometimes a combination of all three. Homecoming music was as common to us as the homecoming meal. Not to have music as part of the celebration was unthinkable. From time to time it might be an individual rendition where someone in the family would sit at the piano and strike out a tune, or it might be group singing of the great hymns of the faith. From every quarter of the house there would come singing—soprano from the kitchen where a cake was being iced, alto from the dining room where the table was being set, tenor from the back porch where shoes were being shined, and bass from the pianist himself. Everybody joined in because everybody was rejoicing that we were all together again. It was the natural overflow of our spirits.

Coming home from college was the same. I can still picture in my mind's eye Mother playfully dancing across the living room to the singing of her own voice. Sometimes, as she was walking through the kitchen on her way to some other part of the house, she would, upon hearing a certain song on the radio, turn her walking into a parody of silliness, as the rest of the family, one by one, would begin to file along behind her throughout the entire house, occasionally winding up in the backyard where we'd collapse, weak with laughter. All of this behavior was the result of somebody she loved coming home for a brief visit.

Back to our story. The Prodigal Son had returned to the father and it was the happiest reunion of his life. There had been a warmly affectionate welcome, feasting, and merrymaking—all characteristic of celebrating home a loved one. Note, if you will, one final thing about the homecoming. It is a bit abstract, but just as important as all the rest. More than the reunion itself it has to do with something that happened before—that period of separation from the younger son, whom the father loved.

See in the Scripture account where the older son, in anger, confronts the father? He reminds his father that he has served him faithfully for many years. He has obeyed his commands. He's done everything he should as an obedient son and yet his younger, wayward brother, who has wasted his money and spent all his time and energies in riotous living, comes home and gets this royal treatment. What's the deal? Why the "favoritism"? There is understandable resentment here, is there not? The father could have said, upon the younger son's return, "Look, kid—it's all over between us. You blew it! I gave you your inheritance and you went away and wasted it. All of it. You've been living like a pig, acting like a pig, looking like a pig, and now you even smell like a pig. Get out of my sight. As far as I'm concerned, I have only *one* son, and it's not you. It's your older brother. He's all I have now in the way of offspring. You've been replaced by him."

That would have been a justifiable reaction, would it not? He could have felt he had the emotional right to replace that vacant spot in his heart by one who was more "worthy," couldn't he? The younger son had been a disappointment to the father. He had squandered all that the father ever gave him and spurned all that the father ever taught him. He could have easily filled the gap in his life with the son of whom he was proud and who had obeyed him all those years. But, the truth is, he didn't! He never gave the older son the younger son's spot. He simply left that vacancy unfilled.

That is important, because the communication bonds that lie between the person who is waiting and the one who is away are kept alive and vital. The spot that is vacant *no one* else can fill. Nor should it be filled. The vacancy itself is what keeps the love, prayers, concern, and hope alive, even at the expense of all the anguish and anxiety. During those weeks, or possibly months or years of separation, some of life's most difficult but meaningful lessons are learned. We must purposely not fill that hole in our heart with somebody else. That spot belongs to "the younger son." The older son had his own place in the father's heart and the two are not interchangeable. One could not be a substitute for the other.

> Nothing can fill the gap when we are away from those we love, and it would be wrong to try and find anything. We must simply hold out and win through. That sounds very hard at first, but at the same time it is a great consolation, since leaving the gap unfilled preserves the bonds between us. It is nonsense to say that God fills the gap; he does not fill it, but keeps it empty so that our communication with another may be kept alive, even at the cost of pain.[2]
>
> Dietrich Bonhoeffer

We've come full circle in talking about celebrating reunions. We've reviewed a classic example in Scripture of what is involved—the open demonstration of affection, the use of our best resources, the value and affects of merrymaking with music. We've even considered the importance of leaving open spaces in our hearts for those we love who are away from us, reminding ourselves that no person who is on the scene can replace another who is off the scene. "Out of sight, out of mind" is only a myth. Everybody has his own spot, carved out only for him.

The next time you're anticipating the homecoming of a loved one, go all out for a welcoming celebration. Make it a joyous and memorable occasion, and let the whole world know how much that special person means to you!

- Meet him or her at the airport, train or bus station, or pier with flowers in hand and a giant bear hug.

- Make a big banner to hang across the living room and decorate your home with balloons, streamers, and confetti.

- Prepare a delectable and aromatic meal, set the table with your best linen, china, crystal, and silver, and eat by candlelight, enjoying each other's company. Kill the fatted calf.

- Set aside private lodgings for your guest (a quiet bedroom, a separate bath with your best towels, perfumed soap, and plenty of bubble bath).

- Leave out his or her favorite records, books, and magazines to be perused at will.

- Plan a picnic or make reservations at an elite restaurant.

- Spend at least one evening listening to music and singing old favorites.

- Drag out the photo albums or college yearbooks and reminisce.

- Grant free run of the house, including the kitchen, for him or her to do whatever whenever.

- Secretly tuck a card or note into packed bags just before your loved one leaves again expressing your joy, adoration, and thankfulness for the special friendship you have, and to let him or her know how much you cherish the fun and fellowship the two (or three or four) of you share.

Celebrate your loved ones home. Turn on all the love lights, brighter than ever before. Make them know they've not been replaced by anyone else. It'll be an occasion you'll never forget . . . and neither will they.

# 6

# Celebrating

# Knowledge

## LEARNING
## FOR THE FUN
## OF IT

From time to time I am asked the question, "What is your favorite thing to do?" I have asked many others the same question because I'm interested in people, and how they answer that question reveals a lot about who they are. I'm always curious to see what we might have in common. Out of the myriad of activities I find delight in, there are three things that would rank right at the top of the list:

1. Visiting with somebody I love,
2. Attending live theater or concerts,
3. Learning something new while having a good time.

It is number three that I want to talk about in this chapter. I love to learn and love to have a good time, and if the two can go together in some way, I am, of all people, most happy!

By reading this far into the book, you have seen that there is no question about my wanting to have a good time. I love having fun, doing things just for the fun of it. Fun makes life more enjoyable. It makes the hard times more endurable. It takes the sting out of loneliness. It adds zest to everyday drudgery and duty. And, it certainly makes learning more exciting, whether it's in a group situation or on one's own. If we can see the fun of something and participate in it, the learning situation has much more overall appeal.

I've had teachers whose techniques and methods made me want to rush to class and not miss a single day of school. They possessed the skill to make even the deadliest facts and figures come to life in a new way. I hated to see each class come to an end because I was having such fun. On the other hand, I've also had teachers or professors (and so have you) whose classes were so everlastingly boring that I would rather have bamboo shoots shoved up my fingernails than go in there. "May the Lord return before the class starts," I would pray. I, the fledgling student, probably could have taught the class better than the knowledgeable professor. What was the difference in the first classroom experience and this one? One teacher knew how to make knowledge inviting and exciting and the other didn't. It's as simple as that in the basic analysis.

I am a firm believer in the fact that learning, for all of us, can be a time of celebration, of fun. My educational theory is based on a philosophy of common sense, with four parts: the sense of scope, the sense of mission, the sense of perspective, and the sense of enthusiasm. These are four rather heavy-duty words, but don't let them scare you. Each one can occur on a daily basis as we learn *anything* new. Let's look at them individually. As we move along, try to put yourself into the category at hand and see how well you fit, in your joy or lack of it, in certain learning situations.

*The Sense of Scope:*

In 1982 I wrote a book entitled, *Wide My World, Narrow My Bed,* with a subtitle, "Living and Loving the Single Life." The book conveys the underlying principle that to have and enjoy a full life as a single person, one needs continually to widen one's world, reach beyond one's own doorstep, look outside the immediate. I felt I could address that issue since I have chosen to remain single all my life.

The same is true with one's pursuit of knowledge. We must realize the world is an enormous place, and everything we do to create a worldwide view broadens our horizons and our choices for living and learning. Expanding our scope of thinking makes life more fun.

Ask yourself, "How wide is my world? Does it reach farther than my own family? Does it go outside my own church boundaries? Does it open up to people and places that are different from what I've always known or been taught? Does it include even one single person of another race or from another country?" Or, is your world narrow in its scope, restricted in its consciousness, limited in its horizons, so that, in effect, you have created a little universe that is much, much smaller than the real world actually is? It is very easy— all too easy, in fact—to exist in a confined, self-centered world. It's safe there. No risks. No involvement. But, no fun either! It can be likened to being sick. When we are sick, our horizons shrink—whether that's physical, mental, emotional, or spiritual sickness. Perhaps you've experienced that.

About five years ago, I was forced to have major surgery and my world became much smaller. Indeed, the sicker I became, the more I circumscribed and restricted my thinking. Some days I simply could not reason beyond my own body and its most elemental needs and functions. For a period of time, I lost interest in the people I knew and loved, in the daily news, in the world at large. I talked about *me* and *my* body and *my* pain, because *my* world had become all I thought about. I lived in one room with one thought: *myself.*

I'll never forget the first day I went outside to go to the doctor's office after five weeks of solitary recuperation and limited thinking about my own little world. Slowly, I walked out my front door onto the porch and encountered something I wasn't ready for— the real world. Everything looked so ominous and massive and scary and just plain different. It reminded me of the poet's view:

> Great wide, beautiful, wonderful world,
> With the wonderful waters round you curled,
> And the wonderful grass upon your breast,
> World, you are beautifully drest.[1]

Although the poet was attempting to capture the essence of beauty in words, I took the meaning very differently at that moment. To me, it expressed the expansiveness of the world. I found myself, somehow, wanting to reduce what I saw outside, to that little world with which I had become familiar inside. The world was too big and too wide for me to face. I had forgotten how it was out there because my scope of thinking had become defined by four walls, and even at times, by the perimeter of the skin around my own body. I slowly began to realize once again that part of the joy of being alive was broadening my horizons. I had to train myself anew with the truth that my sense of scope was directly related to my desire to grow and learn. The following captures exactly what I'm trying to say:

> If illness is the principle enemy of growing, and our expanding horizons, education is its principle ally. For example, through geography, we become conscious of a world as large as the world. Through history, we become conscious of a world as far back as recorded time. Through prophecy, as far ahead as we can imagine. Through philosophy, we become conscious of the unseen world of ideas. Through atomic physics and science, our world expands to include the sub-particles of our very being. Through astronomy, our world expands to include the universe and the stars.[2]

There's no limit to widening our world! Isn't that great? Learning is fun. Learning is the noble challenge of broadening our scope.

Nothing attests to that better than pursuit of trivia that has swept across America. *Everyone* is playing one trivia game or another. And what are they? Nothing more than learning while having a good time. Some of us may be better at trivia than others—and part of the sport lies in the effort to win, of course—but basically, the fun is in the test of our own powers to remember facts and the joy of realizing we actually can (on occasion) call these facts to mind. Out of the limited categories from which to choose, surely there's *something* we know!

In the game of life, however, there are unlimited

categories to pursue. That's even better. Develop for yourself your own goals toward learning and expanding your scope in the various categories which interest you.

- Check out cruises and travel packages and go to that exotic place you've always dreamed about.
- Read at least one new book a month—a classic, a new release from a favorite author, a how-to manual, a biography, the history of a country, new scientific or theological works.
- Try a new way of doing an old job.
- Take a risk. Go out on a limb. Be daring and adventurous.
- Listen to another kind of music. Most libraries have a vast selection of practically every genre of music which you can check out, from classical to country to jazz to rock. Attend an opera or the symphony.
- Enroll in a class—learn a new language, take an arts and crafts course, learn to sail or swim or play tennis or square dance, study the development of English literature, take a course in economics to help you manage a budget at home. The possibilities are endless.
- Open your heart to new people, places, things, ideas. Consider a fresh concept.
- Subscribe to a world news magazine or two (such as *Life, Newsweek,* or *Time*). Keep up on current events.
- Laugh. As Abraham Lincoln once said, "If I did not laugh I should die."
- Put theory into practicality. Challenge yourself to get involved in a cause you believe in.
- Be brave. Reach out. Get up and get at it.

Terence White, in his book, *The Once and Future King,* encourages us *all* to expand our horizons:

"The best thing for being sad," replied Merlin, beginning to puff and blow, "is to learn something. That is the only thing that never fails. You may grow old and trembling in your anatomies, you may lie awake at night listening to the disorder of your veins, you may miss your only love, you may see the world about you devastated by evil lunatics, or know your honor trampled in the sewers of baser minds. There is only one thing for it then—to learn. Learn why the world wags and what wags it. That is the only thing which the mind can never exhaust, never alienate, never be tortured by, never fear or distrust, and never dream of regretting. Learning is the thing for you. Look at what a lot of things there are to learn—pure science, the only purity there is. You can learn astronomy in a lifetime, natural history in three, literature in six. And then, after you have exhausted a million lifetimes in biology and medicine and theocriticism and geography and history and economics, why, you can start to make a cartwheel out of the appropriate wood, or spend fifty years learning to begin to learn to beat your adversary at fencing. After that you can start again on mathematics until it is time to learn to plough."[3]

We're going to run out of lifetimes before we run out of categories of pursuit, aren't we? But, in the meantime, we'll have a heck of a lot of fun! There's no end to the avenues of exploration and study. The limits lie only in our own prejudices or nearsightedness.

### The Sense of Mission:

The philosopher Nietzsche once said, "He who has a *why* to live for can bear with almost any *how.*" That wise statement is very applicable when we think of having a sense of mission. The more we know and the more we learn, the greater the realization of the purpose and aim for our lives. A major part of the joy of living is knowing why we're here in the first place. It's what makes life effective. The *why* that we live for helps us choose how we spend our time, establish our goals, plan our course of study, and invest our energies toward a certain objective. Whatever drives us onward with a kind of sacrificial, burning passion reflects our mission and determines our level of involvement. In this area we become the most creative and innovative because the force that answers to the *why* within us can put up with almost any *how,* always designing new and different ways to hit the bull's-eye of our desire. Nothing seems too hard or too expensive or too time-consuming because what we want to do overcomes all those obstacles that appear to stand in the way.

Our formal education—that is, grade school, junior high, high school, and possibly four years of college—includes the teaching of concepts, theories, skills, and ideas, all designed to help us become basically self-reliant. While this course of study enables us to depend on what we have been taught in school to get a job, it doesn't necessarily teach us how to think for ourselves. Nor does it teach us how to make decisions or handle conflicts or take risks with other people or raise our children or determine our basic goals, objectives, and philosophy of life. Self-reliance cannot dictate our quality of living. Only self-development can do that, and *that* kind of education is a lifelong process. We're never too old to better develop ourselves. We're never too old to focus in more discerningly on our mission.

I read in a newspaper several years ago about a black man in Florida who enrolled in school to learn how to read. The article said he was interested in making a careful study of the Bible to help him become a better preacher. There was a picture of him with an open Bible in front of him. His face revealed all the expectancy and excitement of this new pursuit in his mission for life. And surprise—he was 110 years old! How about that for continuing self-development?

The knowledge required in determining our purpose in living is not necessarily nor essentially found in the classroom, however. Much can be gleaned from our own personal reading of the classics, literature, history, civilization, and certainly an indepth study of God's Word. We can derive great insight into our own lives and where we "fit" in civilization by visiting art or science museums, comparing cultures, attending theater. We can ask ourselves questions about our system of values, questions like:

- What do I really want out of life?
- What makes me happy?
- To what or whom am I utterly committed?
- Do I have peace of mind? If not, why not?
- Am I having fun in life?
- What do I enjoy doing most?
- What are my strengths? My weaknesses?

Then, just for fun, we can try to deal with some of our answers, always searching for the core of who we are so we can determine the area of our mission. I promise you—with a few sessions of that, you'll invent your own game and call it "Important Pursuit."

Purpose, or mission, is determined by the development of values, balance, ethics, humor, morality, and sensitivities. It manifests itself in the way we look at life. The learning processes involved are more intangible than in structured classroom situations; consequently they are usually more fun. To find a sense of mission and celebrate the knowledge of that discovery is confirmed in experiences and feelings such as these:

- Being content with inner quality rather than outer quantity.
- Making choices, then taking responsibility for the consequences of those choices.
- Saying "yes" to involvement more often than "no."
- Becoming devoted to a cause outside ourselves.
- Realizing that no matter who we are or what our calling, we *do* make a difference.
- Committing ourselves to loving and charming people into the kingdom of God, not browbeating them into it.

So now the sixty-four thousand dollar question is, "How do we get there?" How do we achieve a *why* to live for? How do we develop a sense of mission?

I would say in two ways. First, we comprehend that because it is a philosophy of life, we will be learning and working on it for as long as we live. We stop expecting to graduate to a state of "having arrived." We will never arrive, but by being in the pursuit, we cannot help but get nearer our goal. Second, we seek to understand the value of daily events so that we attain an overall meaningful attitude toward life and our particular purpose in it. This leads us right into the third common sense issue.

*The Sense of Perspective:*

The best definition of perspective I ever read was in an advertisement in *Business Week* magazine. It said,

Perspective is the ability to see the forest *and* the trees. To see each part in its relation to the whole. Perspective is the ability to see when a trend is, in reality, a fad; and when the road most traveled is not necessarily the path to take. Perspective is more than applied experience. More than simply seeing more. It is driven by a vision of knowing *what* to look for. And supported by the confidence that comes from having the depth of talents needed to produce results. It is a view from the high ground of objectivity . . . along with a healthy disregard for the impossible.[4]

There is very little in the educational system, categorically, that teaches us perspective. I wish there had been such a class when I was in college—"The Fine Art of Perspective 101"—which, if taken, taught the student how to integrate into the scheme of things when he or she got out into the big bad world. I wish I had received instruction on decision-making. I wish I had realized that some things were relative only to that given situation, and others were absolutely here to stay. I wish somebody had taught me, "Hey, don't sweat the little things. They're only pertinent to this stage of life or this age or this circumstance. Tomorrow it will be different. It'll be something else, something new to worry about, so relax!" Nobody ever taught me that. Oh, I'm learning it. But, it's through experience, not through schooling. Having perspective about life and its problems is the byproduct of experience; it is part of the maturation process, not the educational system. If somebody would have just told me *that* much, it would have helped.

As I've grown older, life has taught me that I am not the center of the universe. Everything doesn't revolve around me. When we're kids (and this is true of all of us, I think) we get the mistaken notion that activities other than our own are secondary to what is truly important. We have tunnel vision. No perspective! Because our world is so narrow, dictated by our limited knowledge and lack of intuition, we cannot see our part in life.

We cannot perceive our relation to the whole of things because of our self-centeredness and immaturity. This is not necessarily a fault; it is a fact, generally characteristic of youth. Lack of perspective is typical of the adolescent, and although a pain in the neck to be around, we sort of hem and haw, practically expecting it from a person who is not yet grown up. The unfortunate thing is that there are countless millions of people who go through their entire *lives* without perspective, from cradle to grave. Unable to see the forest *or* the trees, they see only themselves. They are always subjective, never objective, and they cause misery to everybody else because life revolves only around them.

A few years ago I ran across a book about one of my favorite conductors, entitled *The Private World of Leonard Bernstein*. It was full of photographs, anecdotes about Bernstein and his family, interviews, and his thoughts on various aspects of music in particular and life in general. At one point, Bernstein addresses the idea of egomania in all good artists and how believing in one's self means believing in one's function as being absolutely and inextricably woven with the destiny of the world, of being essential, all-important, and so forth. He said that there was a time when, if he were asked, "What's important?" he would have answered, "I'm important because of what I do and what I'm contributing to the world, for whatever reason." Let me say here as an aside that I agree with that statement primarily. I don't consider it one that needs qualifiers *as long as it's in the right perspective.* But he then added the following, which I found to be an excellent amplifying comment and one that affected me deeply:

> But I find it increasingly difficult to think in those terms. I'm sure that when I was in my twenties I felt that way, that the sun rose and set in my coming and going. The painful process of growing up is simply the constant, ever-widening realization that you are not the center. It's painful. That's why adolescence is painful. Maturing is a painful process.[5]

How true. Too soon old, too late smart!

The Bible is a remarkable commentary on perspective. Through its divine message we are brought face to face with issues and tests in daily living and how, by the power of the Holy Spirit, we are enabled to respond positively to them. In that timeless volume we read about things that happen in our twentieth century world. From its pages we are instructed how to cope with or react to our problems in the proper perspective. It addresses issues involving humility, waiting, suffering, self-centeredness, loss, adversity, prosperity, loneliness, fear, . . . *all* of the things that get us down. Without this perspective, we make ourselves (and everybody else) miserable because we think we are the apex upon which the world turns. We think the sun rises and sets in our coming and going. Generally, when we live out our lives in that cocoon we are not only a disappointment and a trial to be with, but we are impoverished and ineffectual as well. The proper perspective creates within us a spirit of reaching outside of ourselves with joy and enthusiasm.

*The Sense of Enthusiasm:*

You know why I think it's such fun to learn something new? Because with every tidbit of information I get under my belt, it opens yet another door to a different adventure. It's never-ending! It introduces me to a multitude of fresh ideas and different ways of viewing circumstances and life as a whole. It makes me ask even more questions. It makes me enthusiastic about what's going to happen next. You see, real ongoing, lifelong education doesn't answer questions—it provokes them. It causes us to see that the fun and excitement of learning doesn't lie in having all the answers. It lies in the tension and the stretching of our minds between all the contradictory answers. It makes us think for ourselves. It frees us. It helps us grow up! That's where the fun comes in, where those surges of enthusiasm lie. That's where meaningful education takes place.

Even Scripture doesn't tell us every single thing we'd like to know. While it serves as a standard for living and a chart for life's course, much of it remains a secret. God designed it that way and that's okay. In fact, recently I heard my brother Chuck say during one of his Insight for Living broadcasts, "I find myself very comfortable when I come to Scripture that doesn't answer everything." I do too. That keeps us dependent upon God and having to live by faith. Fun, isn't it? And the fun's never going to stop!

When I was a sophomore in college I knew the answers to practically everything in life, but nobody asked me any questions. Now that I'm in my fifties, with all this gray hair and wrinkled skin, I know the answers to practically nothing and people ask me lots of questions. I suppose it's because I finally learned to view life with a sense of scope, a sense of purpose, a sense of perspective, and I'm enthusiastic about all of it. It's been thirty years since I graduated from college, yet in so many ways I realize I've only *begun* to learn how to really live. And, I go on, day after day, being an avid student of life. I have, however, finally figured out how to truly celebrate knowledge. Learn something new every day, just for the sheer fun of it.

# 7
# Celebrating Work

## BALANCING
## THE
## NINE TO FIVES

Thus far, the topics we have considered in terms of celebration have been enjoyable pursuits—savoring the moment, delighting in birthdays, mealtimes, and reunions, reveling in fellowship with our friends and families, and even relishing the joys of learning—both in formal education and just for the fun of it. All of these have been somewhat instinctive in our desire to celebrate because they follow the natural course of what gratifies us without a lot of effort. However, when we come to the idea of celebrating work, that's another story. Or, at least that's the tale most of us have been taught. We've grown to believe these cliches:

- Watch out for ambition! It can get you into a lot of hard work.
- The thing most of us don't like about work is that it's so daily.
- Work is the annoyance people have to endure between coffee breaks.
- The trouble with getting to work on time is that it makes the day so long.
- Never buy anything with a handle on it. It might mean work!

I saw a good one several months ago when I was standing at a public counter in a nearby city hall. It was typed on a small card and taped to the wall:

*If you don't believe in the resurrection of the dead, stick around here till 5 P.M.*

Many of us embrace the idea that work is an affliction, a drudgery, a crushing burden against society which deforms us and holds us back from being all we could be if we just didn't have to report to a job. If labor were reduced (or preferably, eliminated altogether), life would be richer and sweeter. This seems to be the outlook of the majority. At least that has been my discovery as I have chatted with people almost everywhere I've traveled. To most, work is a drag!

There also exists the extreme opposite viewpoint: Work is not a curse, it is humanity's greatest blessing. Were it not for the virtue of work, all our idleness would be wasted or misspent in such a fashion that we would be in constant trouble or mischief. If a person doesn't work, he or she becomes slovenly in habits, behavior, and appearance. The people who think this way live by these homilies:

- It's simply fantastic the amount of work you can get done if you don't do anything else.
- The workman has to perform for his subsistence— night and day.
- You can often gauge a man's ambition by whether he hates his alarm clock or considers it his dear friend.
- A woman's work is never done, from rising dawn to setting sun.
- If you think you work harder than the average worker, you're an average worker.

My question is, "Why can't there be a happy medium?" Surely there is an enjoyable way of accomplishing the tasks before us—whether that's in an office, in a store, in sports, or in school. Wherever we find ourselves employed, whenever we have a job to do, uniform principles should apply which create a balanced life. Our job should be one where our labor produces dignity, self-respect, and an attitude of happy diligence. We need to stop looking at work as simply a means of earning a living and start realizing it is one of the elemental ingredients of making a life! I like the words of Aristotle:

Amusement is needed more amid serious occupations than at other times, for he who is hard at work has need for relaxation, and amusement gives relaxation.

Ah! Now we're beginning to get the picture—the balance I'm talking about. Remember that "scripture" which says, "All work and no play makes Jack a dull boy?" Well, maybe it's not Scripture, but it's close enough to be given credence. And it's true—all work and no play does make one dull. It's terrible! Workaholics are probably the most uninteresting people I know. Crashing bores. All they can talk about is work, and just because they burn the candle at both ends doesn't mean they're all that bright. By the same token, however, the sluggard is equally as dull. Lacking in ambition, these individuals are a pain and a drain on society. When you see them work you wonder what they'll do when they retire, if they make it to retirement. Actually, they're dead now, but won't lie down.

I want us to look at the amusements to which Aristotle refers that create a relaxed atmosphere. To illustrate what constitutes a balance in the duties of a work day, I decided to interview a young man with whom I work at Mobil Oil Corporation, who communicates these principles of balance in his life as well as anyone I know. Joe is his name. Joe is twenty-six, single, very athletic, and good-looking. A college graduate, Joe is a civil engineer, a hard worker, a fine Christian, and a fun, crazy, upbeat guy as well as a first-rate gentleman. If this were not enough, Joe is also an excellent cartoonist and caricaturist. For instance, he has presented individual departments, within the company, drawings of their employees, in the setting (he feels) which best depicts that department's function at Mobil. These exaggerated likenesses have been a source of laughter and the building of camaraderie among all of us. You can get an idea of my department, for example, in the drawing he did for us, which I've reproduced here with Joe's permission.

As Manager of the Rights of Way Department for Mobil's West Coast Pipe Lines, it is among my responsibilities to obtain necessary signatures on various legal

documents. In the drawing, I'm standing in the middle, holding the unsigned document, with pen in hand, imploringly waiting for signatures, flanked by my two agents, Ken with a machine gun and Ruth with a bomb. Our department means business! I asked Joe how he got such an idea for this caricature for the Rights of Way Department, and he told me:

"I looked at the group as a whole and tried to picture how the world viewed a large oil corporation, or at least their Rights of Way section."

"Thanks a lot, kid. Poor Ken with a machine gun and Ruth with a bomb."

"Now wait a minute, Luci. That's not to say the world looks at you as though you're Ma Barker." He went on,

"I think the world views big oil companies or any Rights of Way Department as a threat. I've heard stories of Rights of Way personnel going to see landowners who are holding guns and rocket launchers and everything else. When the owner says, 'Get off my land,' you're ready for 'em! Rights of Way people have to think ahead. I drew you as one who was out to get as much land for the company as possible . . . whether that's with a gun or a bomb. I tried to show your department as the opposite of what you're really like. That's the whole idea of a caricature sketch."

I had the original cartoon framed and it hangs by my desk where I enjoy it daily. Ruth and Ken also have prints and theirs are hanging in their offices as well. It's amazing how Joe captured our looks—perhaps a bit more than we'd like to admit. When we first saw the drawing I asked, "Am I that old?" Ken asked, "Am I that fat?" And Ruth asked, "Do I dress that badly?" You can see where our priorities lie!

I want to tell you about my interview with Joe. As you read this dialogue, keep in mind that both Joe and I spring from an office format, of the "nine to five" variety (or, in our case, seven to four). Whether you are in the same sort of environment or not doesn't matter. The principles are the same. What emerges out of this exchange points up valuable lessons in establishing an atmosphere of balance between hard work and relaxation.

Joe and I recently went out to lunch together and here are the highlights of our conversation:

LUCI: Joe, how do you account for your great spirit about work and your life in general?

JOE: I think happiness is conditional. Basically, I account for the joy in my life as coming from my salvation through Christ. But, a lot of the way I am can be traced back to one of my friends in high school who epitomized what I thought a "fun" Christian should be. This guy's name was Bob Pryor and his statement, "Life

is a total trip," affected me greatly. He lived
life to the hilt.

LUCI: And this guy was a Christian?

JOE: Oh, yeah. You'd love him—he's great! So much
of his attitude about living life fully was passed
on to me.

LUCI: I've been thinking a lot about the idea of celebrating work—something a lot of people are
unable to do. But you seem to do it very well.
You manage to balance your life with hard work
and relaxation on the job! Tell me about that
balance.

JOE: In growing up, I always heard there were two
kinds of people: those who live to work and
those who work to live. I fall into the latter
category.

LUCI: Me too. Actually, I live to eat. Could you pass
the pepper, please?

JOE: But beyond that, I think there are two other
ways to look at work. Number one, we can view
work as something handed down to us, thanks
to Adam, and we are now *forced* to work. It's
something we trudge through every day as a
necessary evil. Or, the second attitude is that
work is an opportunity, another extension of
one's ministry. I favor the second attitude.
When it's our reason for being here, it keeps
us balanced.

LUCI: If one looks at work that way, as part of one's
ministry, do you think that person should witness on the job?

JOE: Well, how do you mean "witness?" You mean
vocally or with actions?

LUCI: Vocally.

JOE: The way I like to witness is to let actions speak
first. If we are consistent in our actions, people
are going to raise questions. When I pray in

the morning before work, I often ask God for the opportunity that day to express vocally what I am (hopefully) showing consistently in my actions. I think people look very harshly and critically at fanatics—those who rush into witnessing or evangelism without really getting to know the other guy. We, as Christians, need to earn the other person's respect; get to know them and show concern in other ways before we witness vocally about what Christ means in our lives.

LUCI: I couldn't agree more, Joe. Do you believe vocal witnessing on the job has a place?

JOE: Yes, I do. But, once again, we initiate opportunities for evangelism by our actions. I stress that because I believe there comes a point when the other person will see the sincerity in our actions and approach us.

LUCI: And you believe we should wait until then?

JOE: In most instances, yes.

LUCI: Let's look at another facet of the work world for a minute. Do you think a Christian employee should behave any differently on the job than a non-Christian? Do we have a greater responsibility for consistent performance than the unbeliever?

JOE: No. People should strive for consistency in every area of life. We shouldn't single out "work" or "play" and be consistent in only one of those areas. Life is a total trip! I think we need to look at the entire picture of our lives and establish consistency in all areas. Employees should be consistent and responsible whether they're Christians or not.

LUCI: Joe, what do you think makes a happy working environment?

JOE: Happy, working people, naturally. That's too

simplistic, but let me explain. A working environment gives the opportunity for people to mix and mingle—to get to know one another, add to each other's lives, see other perspectives on how people think. I'm a "people person." I enjoy people for who they are, often very different from myself. This type of atmosphere helps me confirm or cancel certain attitudes in my own life I might be considering. If I was stuck back in a cave someplace, there are certain people who would not benefit from being around Joe Hancock, and I don't mean that egotistically at all.

LUCI: No, I know what you mean.

JOE: It's that I feel every person has something to give to this world and to other people and the more we reach out and give it and care about others, the more we encourage people to be all they can be. Lifting people up, encouraging and motivating them creates higher values overall in our working environment. That's what makes it happy, I think.

LUCI: A happy work place is one of give and take. Sharing the load. What's your favorite thing about working?

JOE: Oh, the people. No question. I love people and I enjoy being around them. People at work are on a team and I like teams from my years of being in sports.

LUCI: So you don't view your working partners as a family? You view them as a team.

JOE: Right. There's a big difference, too. On a team, everyone retains his own individuality, operating independently from one another, in different areas of strategy but coming together in unity, concentrating in joint efforts toward making Mobil (in our case) the best team in town.

But, I think of a family as involving many more personal aspects of one's life that would be inappropriate in an office. On a team, we are unified in one goal—in a family, there are many goals. When employees enter into a team spirit, work is downright fun.

LUCI: Good point. I hadn't thought of it quite like that. Also, in a family, there is heavy emphasis on parental guidance and supervision, but on a team there's one captain and many members, all in strategic spots. That's important in the work place.

JOE: Oh, yes. Very important. It makes all the difference in that balance you're talking about.

LUCI: Two or three final questions, then we'll close up shop. If a Christian is unhappy on a job, what do you think is the best way to handle that? Should he or she keep quiet about it, learn to live with it, speak up, shut up, quit or what?

JOE: The worst thing is to ignore it. We've been called as Christians into a ministry. Our jobs are a vital part of that ministry and God hasn't called us to a life of drudgery every day, living with doom or gloom over our heads. So, the first thing I'd do is confront God with it. I'd pray about it, asking Him to reconfirm where I'm supposed to be, at that particular point in my life and career. Second, I'd ask trusted friends for advice. I wouldn't even be opposed to going to my supervisor. I have a good relationship with my supervisor, so I'd go to him and say, "Hey, these are my problems," or, "This is why I'm uncomfortable and unhappy in my job," and see what might be done. Be honest. If we're honest with people and they feel our sincerity, usually people are willing to help us. In any event, I wouldn't accept things as they were and let it die there. I'd try to find out what the real problems were and deal with those before I quit. Maybe there would be a good lesson in it. Quitting often means running from one problem to a worse one down the road.

LUCI: Someday, when it's all said and done and the books are written and the royalties are collected and you're old and gray and your wife is a mother of sixty-five, and. . . .

JOE: Sixty-five what?

LUCI: Why, sixty-five children. No, sixty-five years old and your three children are grown, married, and gone from the old homestead, and you're entering retirement after a successful forty years with Mobil, what would you like most to have said of you? "I remember old Joe Hancock and he was a. . . ."

JOE: "Blankety-blank" and you want me to fill in the blanks?

LUCI: Yeah.

JOE: Okay. I would like it said that I gave my best. No. That's a cliché. I'd like people to say I "flavored the work environment" . . . that they enjoyed working with me because I made work fun. If anything, since we as Christians are the salt of the earth, I like the idea of getting out of the salt shaker, into the workplace. Then, we can truly be the flavor, the people who add the spice. The people who add enjoyment to whatever we do. I would consider it a very high compliment if people just said, "Joe Hancock? Oh, yeah . . . I always enjoyed being around that guy."

"Flavor the work environment!" I like that. It succinctly sums up the secret of celebrating work. Joe's overall philosophy captures the hidden but essential ingredients of balancing our Monday through Fridays, our nine to fives. In substance, here's the true picture of the principles of balance Joe has drawn for us. To experience the joy that can rightfully be ours in our work-a-day world, we must:

- Earn other people's respect through our actions, before our words.
- Establish consistency in both responsibility and recreation.
- Enjoy people for who they are in genuine give-and-take.
- Encourage others to be all they can be, by motivation and high values.
- Enter into a winning team spirit with unity toward one goal.

You can't tell me those kinds of attitudes won't win, hands down, every time! That's exactly the basic, overall principle behind the book *In Search of Excellence: Lessons from America's Best-Run Companies,* which preaches:

> The excellent companies have a deeply ingrained philosophy that says in effect, "Respect the individual," "Make people winners," "Let them stand out," "Treat people as adults."[1]

This isn't easy to achieve, nor is it ever accomplished in one fell swoop. It's a process and at the same time, an objective. But, even in the pursuit there is enjoyment and fulfillment. In the difficulties and hardships there lies solidarity, growth and success.

The dictionary is the only place where success comes

before work. But don't miss the hoopla and celebration that's hidden in all that labor. That's where we'll find the amusement "needed more amid serious occupations than at other times." Don't you think it's interesting that the words of Aristotle, written over three hundred years before the birth of Christ, and these words from John Naisbitt and Patricia Aburdene, written in 1985, are saying the same thing? We've come full circle:

Many business people have mourned the death of the work ethic in America. But few of us have applauded the logic of the new value taking its place. "Work should be fun." That outrageous assertion is the value that fuels the most productive people and companies in this country . . . In their hearts, people *know* that work should be fun and that it should be related to the other parts of their lives.[2]

Let's finalize it with this realistic "everyday" picture:

"Success is a journey, not a destination." Happiness is to be found along the way, not at the end of the road, for then the journey is over and it is too late.
Today, this hour, this minute, is the day, the hour, the minute for each of us to sense the fact that life is good, with all its trials and troubles, and perhaps more interesting because of them.[3]

# 8

# Celebrating

# Accomplishments

## COMMEMORATING THE VICTORY

Several years ago a fabulous little book came out called *The No Choice Diet.* It was exactly what the title implied—a stick with it, strict, do-exactly-as-outlined diet that, when rigidly followed, guaranteed the loss of ten pounds in thirty-three days. Definitely written for the no-nonsense dieter who meant business about losing weight. I bought the book and set out upon my thirty-three day venture toward being more fit than fat . . . and it was fun. I made long lists of food to buy, cooked dishes I had never prepared before, bought a new nonstick skillet, graphically kept track of my weight loss on a homemade chart stuck to the refrigerator, exercised religiously, and watched those pounds drop off somewhere under my digital scale every time I hopped on it. No more did I get the little computer print-outs from the scale that read, "Come back when you're alone." I did indeed lose ten pounds in thirty-three days, just as the book promised.

Of course, as is true with any diet, there were times I hated it and was ready to pull my hair out by the roots. I was always having to measure every morsel, never deviating from what was prescribed. No candy bars. No Ma Maison. No cake or french fries or foreign delicacies. It was a pain in the neck. But I did like the results. And, as a whole, I liked the diet itself. One of the main reasons was that in the introductory section of the book there was a paragraph entitled "Reward Yourself." That was great advice! At the loss of three pounds, for instance, I was supposed to give myself a present. Nothing big, just some remembrance of the event. A "little trophy," I called it. When I lost five pounds, I would get another present. Then, at eight pounds, a third. The idea was that all along the way I was supposed to be rewarding my accomplishments with celebrations. The achievement trophies spoke of the realization of an anticipated goal. These gifts to myself were the symbols of favorable execution of performance. Naturally, the gift-giving time became my favorite part of the whole diet because of what it said to me: "You did it, woman! You lost that weight. You accomplished your goal. Now, get out there and celebrate with a trophy." I even remember my rewards:

Three pounds  –  a fancy thermos
Five pounds  –  a picnic basket
Eight pounds  –  a haircut and new hairstyle

Ten pounds  –  a tailored business suit and
blouse (one size smaller!)

There's only one thing the book advocated that I
didn't follow. As an incentive toward completion, each
page, when read and fulfilled, was to have been torn
out and thrown away. That meant you had passed that
day. I never did that. Somehow, I liked seeing where
I had come from. It helped me measure the miles I
had traveled from day one and it reminded me of all
it took to get there. Looking at all that discipline of
those past pages gave me courage in other areas in
my life, too, where I had set goals. My conscious mind
was telling my subconscious, "If you can accomplish
*this*, you can also accomplish *that*, so keep going."
British prime minister Benjamin Disraeli once said:

The secret of success is constancy to purpose.

Oh, the joy of accomplishment! Aim for a goal and
stick to it. And when you reach that goal, the natural
result is to celebrate. We like to finish things, don't
we? And to absolutely *know* we've finished, there's
nothing like beating the drums, popping the corks,
throwing the confetti, and commemorating the victory.
If we realize a celebration is down the road, it makes
the road easier to travel. The tests along the way are
easier to bear. Personally, I find I am more willing to
defer rewards when I anticipate a big event at the
end of the journey. That event serves as an incentive
toward which I aim. It is part of the "spoils of victory."
I love that thought. Many a time it has kept me going
when all other inducements were dropping by the way-
side. People were no longer cheering me on. My initial
enthusiasm was waning. I was tired or discouraged.
But there was that trophy of victory at the end of the

race, out on the horizon of my venture. That trophy gave me the inspiration I needed to continue, so on I would go.

Rewards are the touchstones in our lives—physically, materially, academically, financially, and even spiritually. They affirm our growth and the alchemy of our hearts.

Isn't "victory" a wonderful word? Especially when it applies in your own life? Victory has been defined as "achievement in a struggle against odds or difficulties." It means *winning.* Look for a minute at some of the occasions in your past where you've been victorious in a pursuit or struggle, and you celebrated when it was over (or should have if you didn't):

- Report cards
- Ball games
- Job promotions
- Graduation from school
- Losing weight
- Paying off a debt
- Starting a business
- Writing a book
- Anniversaries
- Retirement

There are dozens more victories in your life which you can name, too. Didn't you feel relieved and ecstatic at the same time once that specific goal was attained? You're a winner, a success, a victor!

In the Bible, there are many accounts of celebrating accomplishments. But the one that first comes to mind took place in the life of King David, found in 2 Samuel 6.

Dust it off and read that whole chapter. It will be some-what out of context with the entire picture, but I'll give you a little background to go on.

Prior to chapter 6 David had been crowned king of Israel (he was already king of Judah). The Philistines hated him for this and had tried to capture him. Battles took place, but the Lord God honored the king of Israel and poured out kindness upon His chosen people, the Israelites. When David had defeated the Philistines, he organized his troops to bring the ark of the covenant home to Israel. The ark housed the tablets of the law and served as a symbol of the presence of the living God. It had been missing from its rightful place for seventy years, having been taken by the Philistines. David was determined it would once again be in the center of the kingdom of God's people, so after his victory, he brought the ark home. Verse 12 reads:

> . . . he brought the Ark to the City of David with great celebration. After the men who were carrying it had gone six paces, they stopped and waited so that he could sacrifice an ox and a fat lamb. And David danced before the Lord with all his might, and was wearing priests' clothing. So Israel brought home the Ark of the Lord with much shouting and blowing of trumpets (TLB).

In other words, David was commemorating the vic-tory! The goal had been accomplished and it was time to celebrate, to dance, to shout, to blow trumpets. There was a sacrifice made, which was characteristic for David's day. We don't offer animal sacrifices any-more because that was under another time frame in God's economy. But we do offer the sacrifice of praise to God, as Hebrews 13:15 tells us. We thank Him for what He does by praising His name and telling others of the glory of His greatness. That's all part of the celebration process, so to speak. All of our accomplishments are made possible by the grace and provision of God. There is no better way to praise Him than to "dance before Him" with all our might. It's as though joy flowed out of King David's pores. He couldn't contain himself. Nor should we! Celebrations for accomplishments are definitely in order.

In a recent issue of *Newsweek* I was most interested to read the account of a victory rally headed by the president of the Philippines, Corazon Aquino. This tiny, fifty-three-year-old woman had become the leader of a nation of fifty-five million people because she never retreated. For twenty-eight years of marriage, she was quietly and utterly devoted to her husband until his assassination in 1983. She was never even groomed for political life, always preferring to remain in the shadows of politics, emphasizing her relationship with her family and her faith in God. But then the tables turned. As President Ferdinand Marcos collapsed in his own decay, Aquino went from "just a housewife" to the president of the country.

The article was fascinating to me. It made constant references to her goals—"ordinary goals of a well-bred young lady"—and how she achieved them one by one. It talked of her inner strength, her religious faith, and her fiercely independent will.

Corazon Aquino married a young journalist, Ninoy, who came to the United States to study politics. To join him, she herself had to drop out of law school. After they returned to the Philippines and after she bore him five children, her husband was charged with murder by the Marcos regime and spent seven years in prison. During this period, the family spent Christmas Eves together in the military stockade, sleeping on mattresses on the floor of Ninoy's cell. She said they celebrated by "being together and just pouring our hearts out." One of her husband's sisters had said that the prison years were when the family began to really admire Corazon. Her dedication to her husband and her family was endless.

This was a woman who had all her priorities lined up in order: God, family, country, others. She deferred rewards. She was tenacious on a road that was difficult. She wasn't embarrassed about the place of God in her life. She seemed oblivious to danger, because, as she put it:

> Faith is not simply a patience which passively suffers until the storm is past. Rather, it is a spirit which bears things—with resignation, yes, but above all with blazing serene hope.[1]

I think those are marvelous words of wisdom! From one who has moved from victory to victory with "blazing serene hope," she now has every reason in the world for a victory rally. There *should* be dancing in the street. And there should be joy in the faces of the people, singing, praise, and thanksgiving.

Stop to think over the accomplishments in your life again. Isn't it a great feeling to be able to look back and see how far you've come? But remember, you wouldn't be where you are now if you hadn't set your sights toward a goal and continued to strive for that mark.

Some of the most successful men and women in America attribute their accomplishments to goal setting. Their advice is to sit down, outline your dreams and desires, and make those goals a constant thought. Be daring! Be ambitious! You can't just wait passively hoping something great will happen to you. David had to seek out the Philistines before he could defeat them and bring the ark of the covenant back to Zion. Cory Aquino had to campaign and get the support of the people before she could be elected president. You had to study and pass your tests before you could graduate from school. Be determined to follow your dreams and be prepared to celebrate your accomplishments.

Dr. Robert Schuller is a great advocate of positive thinking. In his bestseller, *The Be-Happy Attitudes,* Dr. Schuller says:

> Are you satisfied? Are you happy? Is life all that you hoped it would be? It can be—it *will* be—if you will say "Yes" to the dream that God has given you.
>
> - Go for it! You might make it!
> - Go for it! It might happen!
> - Go for it! Somebody might be helped by it!
> - Go for it! You might rise from poverty to prosperity!
> - Go for it! If you prosper, you might be able to help the poor!
> - Go for it! Someday, somebody will come to you and say, "Thank you!"[2]

Ask God to show you the plans he has for your life. And once you have an idea what your goal is, don't be afraid to go for it!

If I ever had what some people call "my life's verse" it would be 1 John 5:4 because it addresses the ultimate in celebrating accomplishments:

> For whatever is born of God overcomes the world; and this is the victory that has overcome the world—our faith (NASB).

To accomplish anything of value we must have faith. We must operate by faith from goal to goal. We must walk by faith from day to day. How could David dance before the Lord with all his might? Because his faith paid off. How can Cory Aquino look ahead with blazing serene hope? Because her faith is secure. How can you or I achieve anything in our lives? Faith—our faith in God through Jesus Christ. It overcomes the world. And that's the greatest victory celebration of all!

# 9
# Celebrating

# Imagination

## INVENTING
## THE
## UNINVENTABLE

Imagination is a strange and many-splendored thing. It is the "stuff of which dreams are made." And where would we be without it? Thomas Edison, Wolfgang Amadeus Mozart, Orville and Wilbur Wright, William Shakespeare, Rembrandt and Picasso—the power of their imaginations changed our world.

Walt Disney—now there's a giant imagination for you. Think of the joy and fun it would have been to watch him work, to spend a whole day with him as ideas and concepts rolled out of his head. He once said that Disneyland really began when his two daughters were very young. They called Saturdays "Daddy's Day" and Walt Disney would take them to the park to ride the merry-go-round and play. While sitting alone on a bench eating peanuts and watching his children ride the painted horses on the carousel, he began to envision a kind of family park where parents and children could go to have fun together. His dream ultimately became the wonderful realities of Disneyland in Anaheim, California, and later Disneyworld in Orlando, Florida, two of the most magnificent and enormous amusement parks in the world! Because Disneyland had no precedent, there were no simple or tried-and-true solutions in its design or construction. Every single thing was unique. Isn't that fabulous? It *all* began in Walt Disney's head.

Webster defines imagination as:

> The action of forming mental images or concepts of what is not actually present to the senses; the faculty of producing ideal creations consistent with reality.

I call it "inventing the uninventable." Have you ever stopped to consider that every time you listen to music, turn on your television, read a book, go to a movie or a play or watch a comedian perform, every time you view a painting or a sculpture, it is the product of someone's imagination? Every invention and creation began with a "mental image or concept" of what was not actually present to the senses. As Joseph Conrad puts it:

> Imagination, not invention, is the supreme master of art as of life.

I had the most original and creative roommate some years ago. Nancy had such unique and remarkable ideas that the rest of us just stood around and marveled. As an art teacher in the public school system, she was always on the lookout for new and different ways to decorate her classroom or to encourage her students to be creative. She had an eye for what was yet uninvented, but she could imagine an "ideal creation" from any raw material. And she wasn't afraid to let her imagination run wild.

I vividly recall speeding along in her car one Saturday morning early in December, the two of us chatting our heads off. Suddenly, she made a fast U-turn and drove straight to a big green dumpster. She had spotted four or five huge pieces of cardboard when we drove by and went back to rescue them. Wondering what on earth we were doing, I said, "Nancy, why are we stopping? And in front of the garbage bin . . . what's wrong?"

"Nothing," she responded nonchalantly, as though this were our common Saturday morning custom. "I just saw a manger scene in here and I wanted to pick it up."

"Manger scene?" I asked, peering into the dumpster. "Where? I don't see any manger scene. All that's here are huge pieces of corrugated cardboard boxes."

"Well, it's not a manger scene *yet*," grinned Nancy, "but it will be. It's in this cardboard. All I have to do is make it. I want it for my classroom for Christmas. I've been wondering what I was going to do for my holiday decorations this year, then when I saw this from the highway, it hit me."

So we stacked the big cardboard strips on top of her car and zig-zagged down the road, each of us gripping the edges with one hand to keep the pieces from blowing away in the wind. And over the next week, I watched in amazement as the little town of Bethlehem and a manger scene emerged out of old and dirty strips of corrugated board from a roadside dumpster. It was great! All it took was a pair of scissors, a strong craft knife, a yardstick, some pencils, a few paintbrushes, dirty old cardboard, and bushels of imagination!

That was only one of the countless times Nancy astounded and thrilled me with her inventive prowess. Sometimes I would have to run errands on Saturday morning, and on the way out the door I would shout, "Nance, if you get the urge to make anything while I'm gone, don't. Please wait until I get home so I can watch."

We had many a dinner party where the apartment was lavishly decorated just to suit a particular dish. Once, we invited twenty guests to a Hawaiian luau in our backyard. We converted the clothesline poles into papier-mâché palm trees and ran garlands of greenery along the lines themselves. Leis and grass skirts added to the atmosphere, more evidence of Nancy's unending imagination. Naturally, everyone wanted an invitation to our dinner parties! Nancy was one of the most imaginative people I have ever known, and the genius of her ability brought many friends weeks, months, and years of mesmerizing fascination.

If you are blessed with a creative imagination, use it. Celebrate it! Keep it alive and well-oiled by constantly dreaming of inventions from which others will benefit. You don't have to build a Disneyland, but you can produce creative accomplishments in your own realm. Be imaginative and creative in your planning, during vacations, on your days off, at mealtimes, at parties, in your dress, in your decor. Make your own giftwraps and greeting cards. Invent new recipes. Don't be afraid to let your mind try new ideas. Constantly look for the hidden possibilities in the obvious.

Celebrated artist Pablo Picasso took items that other

people would call "refuse from the local dump" and turned them into works of art worth a small fortune! His advice to would-be artists was to let their imaginations rule:

> We mustn't be afraid of inventing *anything*. . . . Everything that is in us exists in nature. After all, we're part of nature. If it resembles nature, that's fine. If it doesn't, what of it? When man wanted to invent something as useful as the human foot, he invented the wheel, which he used to transport himself and his burdens. The fact that the wheel doesn't have the slightest resemblance to the human foot is hardly a criticism of it.[1]

My friend Marilyn loves to use her imagination to make up details about people. We'll be walking down the street and I'll say, "Mar, tell me about that guy over there at the bus stop."

Without faltering, she'll answer, "That man is from Latvia. He speaks very little English, but enough to get by. He's forty-seven and has always dreamed of coming to America. And now he's here, but he's unemployed and only has $6.35 in his pocket and. . . ."

A vivid imagination can be an endless source of amusement and entertainment. Tap your own resources and see how much fun it can be. Develop your imagination. Try reading more, instead of watching so much television. Even try writing, if that's something you've always wanted to do. Lewis Carroll's *Alice in Wonderland* and Clement Moore's *A Visit from St. Nicholas* were written for the enjoyment of their own children, but they've become immortal works loved by children (and adults) the world over. If you like storytelling, go ahead and spin a few yarns of your own. One guy constantly amuses family and friends with his little ditties about everything from boric acid to crab grass to the dead spider under the kitchen sink.

Once, when I was on yet another diet, I asked Marilyn to help me watch my weight, especially with sweets, for which I have a fatal weakness. During the first couple of weeks, everything went great. Lots of fish, chicken, cottage cheese, and lettuce. But on my way home from work one afternoon, I had an uncontrollable urge to drive by that Baskin-Robbins ice cream parlor near my house. "Life's too short," I thought, "to never have ice cream again." In no time I was lapping around the edge of a large scoop of "chocolate 'n peanut butter" on a lightly toasted sugar cone. Heavenly!

Later that evening, after Marilyn and I did a little shopping, I jokingly asked her if she'd like to stop by the ice cream parlor for a cone. Without the slightest hesitation, she responded, "Great idea! I was just thinking how delicious one would taste right now. Besides, you've been so good all this time, you deserve it. Come on, I'll buy."

As guilty as I felt, I just *couldn't* tell her. We drove along in silence, Marilyn no doubt relishing the idea of savoring ice cream, me praying fervently that the woman who waited on me earlier was no longer on duty. We got our ice cream (a different saleswoman was at the counter) and sat in the car, munching, licking, and making small talk. Then the brilliant idea hit me that it might be fun to confess my sin in some creative way. So I turned to Marilyn and said, "Hey, Mar, if you can tell me what I'm thinking about this Baskin-Robbins store, I'll take you to see that musical we've been wanting to go to."

"What? Is that it? No hints?"

"No hints. You get three guesses. Come on, Mar, you can do it. Just think what I'm thinking."

"Fat chance." I winced when she said that. "Okay,

Luci, my first guess is that you've decided to have your picture made right here in front of the store for your new book. Everybody will see how festive you are and will want to buy the book."

"Great guess! That's fabulous! It's *wrong*, but it's such a good guess!"

After a few more minutes of intense concentration, Marilyn said, "All right. My second guess is that you have made arrangements to work in this ice cream parlor for one week in order to gather stories for your book. Right?"

I grinned back. "Wrong again, pal. But your guesses are so vivid. Shows you're *really* using the ol' imagination."

Suddenly, she blurted out, "This is outrageous, I know, but since I only have one more guess, I'll shoot in the dark. Here's number three: You've already been in here once today for ice cream. Chocolate. You didn't want to tell me earlier because you were embarrassed since you had asked me to help you stick to your diet. And then when I answered 'yes' when you asked if I wanted to come here, you were so caught off guard that you decided to go along with it anyway like nothing had happened. That's why you ordered lemon ice cream. You already had chocolate once today. Besides, lemon is nearer your diet and you thought I'd be proud of you if I heard you order lemon instead of chocolate."

I stared at her with my half-eaten cone poised in midair.

"Well???"

"Marilyn, this is *unreal!* I can't believe it! How did you guess that? *I'm* the only one who could know all those details. Boy is this spooky! A regular Steven Spielberg production."

She was roaring with laughter. It seems that the woman who had waited on me earlier in the day was the mother of a school friend of Marilyn's daughter, Beth. In a casual conversation at the grocery store, the woman innocently mentioned to Marilyn that I had been in that afternoon for an ice cream cone. She had recognized me from church and knew that Marilyn and I were friends. Marilyn decided not to mention the incident to me, but when I made such a big deal about "sticking" to my diet, she thought she'd beat me at my own game. What an imagination that woman has! She played along from start to finish! I loved it!

Let your imagination run wild and think up new ways to add spice to your life. If you like to sew, design your own clothes. If you like to cook, invent your own specialties. If you like to tinker with tools, make your dog a custom-designed doghouse. Train your mind's eye to see "what is not actually present to the senses."

Abigail Van Buren tells the story of a wealthy woman who asked a famous milliner to design a hat for her. He placed a canvas form on the woman's head, and in a matter of eight minutes had created a beautiful hat with a single piece of ribbon, right before her eyes.

The matron was absolutely delighted. "How much will that be?" she asked.

"Fifty dollars," he replied.

"Fifty dollars! Why, that's outrageous," she said. "It's only a piece of ribbon!"

The milliner quickly unraveled the ribbon and, handing it to her, said, "Madame, the ribbon is free."

Don't think that just because you can't make hats out of ribbons or crèches out of old cardboard that you aren't a creative person. Everyone is blessed with an imagination. Some just know how to use it better than others. Developing your imagination takes some effort. Don't quench your creativity with thoughts of "I could never do that," or "That's impossible," or

"Maybe some other day." Let your mind dream big. Brainstorm, just letting your thoughts run rampant. You may even hit on something that will change the world! As Robert Browning wrote in his poem "Andrea del Sarto":

> Ah, but a man's reach should exceed his grasp,
> Or what's a heaven for?

Don't settle for premade, premeasured, prepackaged life. Keep your friends and family guessing what you'll do next. Make life an exciting adventure for you *and* for them!

Some people use their imaginations to allow them to vicariously do the things they've always wanted to do. A few travel brochures or posters and a quiet, shady spot under a big leafy tree are all that are needed for a trip to Paris or Tokyo or Rio de Janeiro. An adventure story is the only thing required to travel back in time or forward in time or even to other planets! Haven't you flipped through a friend's photo album and felt as though *you* actually went to Acapulco, too? That's the power of imagination. Ralph Waldo Emerson once said:

> There are no days in life so memorable as those which vibrated to some stroke of the imagination.

Leo Buscaglia, another supporter of celebrating the spirit of living, puts it this way:

> Imagination is the place where we keep the things that cannot be and yet we know they *are*. We sometimes assume that only children are especially in touch with this magical place, that adults have shed their innocence for a more tangible world. There are the vague recollections of a time in our lives when all things were possible,

when the real world, with all its logic and restraint was not yet upon us. Still, there are those occasional flights of fantasy, the daydreams, the journeys to faraway places. . . . With just a little imagination we can shake loose from the commonplace and make memorable some of those moments that are habitually the same. More and more it seems that life is a creative achievement, something more than just security and comfort. Imagination is being able to envision limitless possibilities and alternatives. It is seeking new solutions to old problems. Each day offers new opportunities, new experiences—no day has ever been like any other, and neither should our approach to it. . . . We have to take responsibility for our own boredom and delve into the limitless opportunities that our imagination affords us. Whether in fashioning a masterpiece of art, or seeing a problem from a new perspective, the creative instinct is uniquely human and waiting within you to be tapped. So when your life seems emptier than it should, when it needs a healthy transfusion of vitality, use your imagination and tap your dreams.[2]

Your imagination is potentially infinite. It can stretch the boundaries of time and circumstances and resources. You can learn to make something out of nothing, to form new concepts and produce "ideal creations." And life is chock-full of opportunities for you to appreciate the inventiveness of others. Tell them how much you enjoy their ability and creativity. Even the most gifted people need encouragement. As affirmation increases, so does creativity. But above all, use your imagination to celebrate life.

Many years after Disneyland was completed, Walt Disney was overheard saying to one of his staff, "The greatest joy of all is the fun I have just watching others have fun." Let's have a party in celebration of imagination—inventing the uninventable. I'll bring the ice cream. You bring the confetti!

# 10
# Celebrating Beauty

## LOOKING FOR THE ESSENCE

$A$ few weeks ago, while I was dusting a shelf of books in my living room, I inadvertently opened the front cover to one of the volumes and read an inscription I had written on the flyleaf many years before. The title of the book was *The Tapestries of Egypt,* and the inscription read, "To my mother . . . the first person to give me an appreciation for beauty. Merry Christmas, 1969." Mother died in 1971 and I kept the book as part of my library and as a reminder of one of her many intangible gifts to me—the gift of appreciating beauty.

My mother was, without doubt, the earliest and most positive influence in my life in that area. Unfailingly, she inspired me to concentrate my focus toward that which would produce the essence of beauty, even when she was unaware of that inspiration. Because of her advice and guidance while I was growing up, I believe it is accurate to say that looking for the essence of beauty is the basic theme upon which my life is strung. Both my general and personal pursuits have been a constant effort to find the clearest expression of what I thought was beautiful in any chosen medium or avenue of communication, beginning with an idea and progressing step by step into the making of a life. I have consciously sought after those things which make for value, order, richness, spirit, and wonder, even though I am often unable to verbalize what I feel when I perceive something beautiful. Sometimes it's a pang or a sensation; at other times it is an awareness of joy and security or pure pleasure. In any event, it is a moment to be celebrated. Beauty justifies itself. The fact that it defies definition means nothing.

What I hope to achieve in this chapter is to point up those characteristics ingrained into beauty which make it what it is, elusive and difficult to explain though it may be. Perhaps when we identify the distinguishing components of beauty, we will realize there are countless moments during the day to celebrate it, to praise God, to recognize that our world of factories and stock reports and guns and monotony is also a world filled with poetry, flowers, and light—beauty. Beauty brings magic and joy as it transforms and transfigures. It may last only a fleeting moment, but in that impermanence itself, beauty derives part of its enchantment. We must train ourselves to capture that passing moment of magic as our own. I think of it like this:

Because of the light of the moon,
Silver is found on the moor;
Because of the light of the sun,
There is gold on the walls of the poor.

Because of the light of the stars,
Planets are found in the stream;
Because of the light in your eyes,
There is love in the depths of my dream.[1]

When a sudden ray of sun or a moonbeam falls on a dreary street, it makes no difference what it illumines—a broken bottle on the ground, a fading flower in a field, or the flaxen blonde hair of a child's head. The object is transformed and the viewer is transfixed. Celebrate that moment of beauty and take it with you in your memory. It is God's gift to you.

There is an old saying: "Man is the measure of all things." This statement was never more applicable than in the realm of recognizing what is beautiful in life. We all measure what is beautiful by the effect things have upon us, according to how they seem to be to us. What seems beautiful to one person may not be to another, or even to the same person at a different time. There is another old saying: "Beauty is in the eye of the beholder." In other words, beauty is subjective or relative to individual judgment and taste. It is never "fixed." No one can question its validity because it is dependent upon the state we are in, not necessarily upon the object we are viewing.

Shortly after I graduated from college with my degree in commercial art, I became friends with a young man who was also a recent graduate in the field of fine art. He had completed his undergraduate work in another college in Texas and had a burning aspiration for further education in Europe. His dream was to go to Paris, France, to live and study "in the shadow of the Louvre." Fortunately, he had carefully saved his money throughout his summers of employment and was able to obtain a visa to live and study abroad—a dream come true!

He packed enough clothes to get by and happily left for Paris the same month I went to work for Mobil Oil. During his stay there he wrote a few letters which perfectly describe the point I want to make. At first, he expressed the romance he enjoyed with his new life. He had secured a little room in the top of a house in Paris and was enthusiastically involved in his art studies and painting. Everything was beautiful! His mansard room had one small square window that over-looked rooftops and pink chimney pots. He could see the *Institut*, the *Pantheon*, and the *Tour Saint Jacques*. Even though some of the floor tiles in the room were broken and got out of place, they added "character" to his quarters. There was a tiny wash basin, a stove, a pitcher, and piles of books, drawings, and prints—his studies. Often, he wrote, he would hang these stud-ies on the bare walls, thus creating the look of his own private gallery or museum. His bed was a small cot. Such a wonderful, romantic place! "Something right out of the first act of *La Boheme*." He loved the look of everything, all the feelings of being a struggling art-ist. He frequently wrote, "It is a beautiful life."

He told me he used to keep Camembert outside the window on the mansard roof and milk in small bottles sat buried in the snow on cold days. He bragged of making fine coffee and discovering new ways to dress up eggs and macaroni. In this haven of beauty and charm my friend thought, made compositions, wrote letters home, and dreamed of his future as a great artist. Doesn't it all sound fabulous? Every time I would read one of those letters I found myself wishing I had fol-lowed my art instructor's advice, "If you have a heart and a shirt, sell your shirt and go to Paris."

And, it *was* fabulous, as long as he looked at everything with those eyes. But the day came when his hopes looked black, his money ran out, and the mansard roof leaked. Then his letters changed. The art student's paradise was turned into a dirty, tiny room with broken tiles. Ashes fell from the stove, the milk soured on the roof, he was tired of Camembert and eggs and macaroni. Everything was hopelessly poor and wretched and there wasn't a shadow of significance in those delicate little chimney pots, the rooftops, the *Pantheon,* the *Institut,* or the *Tour Saint Jacques.*

What happened? The view had not changed. Nor had the room. Nor had my friend's circumstances, really. Even though he was more broke, perhaps, that was nothing new. He had coped with poverty before.

The difference came when he stopped seeing things in correlation and began to view everything from a different perspective. Upon moving into this tiny room, all the surrounding conditions were enhanced by coming into contact with his happy mood—the mood of discovery, the mood of challenge, the mood of romance. In other words, all he saw and did was relative to his emotions. What he needed to remember was that emotions change. Correlation of factors does not continue. Their significance and vitality endure only for a moment, but in that moment lies the beauty. And to recapture it, we must train ourselves to memorize that "vital moment." The celebrating of that moment, then, can repeat itself again and again in our memory as we are able to bring it to our consciousness.

Beauty is a value. That is, it is not the perception of a fact from the will or intellect. It is a quality born of emotions, an affection from our appreciative nature. Shakespeare puts it another way:

Beauty is the cooperation of pleasures.

Looking for the essence of beauty means endeavoring to see that which is better than we know. In a landscape, for instance, it is not just viewing the hills or meadows or waving grass framed against a bright blue sky, but it is capturing the splendor and spirit of the whole. It is seeing the "prose of nature" and taking a picture of that with our mind's camera, the eye, to be focused and enjoyed in our memory forever. Or, when gazing at a lush forest, it is the act of pure contemplation with no regard for wanting anything from the forest. It is allowing ourselves to be immersed in its beauty and color rather than thinking of various trees we might want to cut down or a particular section we might want to buy. When we look into the face of another human being, beauty lies in the discernment of the character of the person and not in the features of the face. Sappho, the Greek poetess who lived six centuries before Christ, states it simply:

> To have beauty is to have only that. But to have goodness is to *be* beautiful too.

Looking for the essence of beauty is comprehending and appreciating that quality in an object which is fairer and better than only what our eyes see or our ears hear—whether that be a Mozart sonata, a painting by Van Gogh, a patch of blue in an overcast sky, the fleeting laughter from a voice we love, or something as unexpected as the rainbow colors in a spot of oil on the driveway. Our world is immersed in the miracles of beauty—enough for several lifetimes—free of charge, if we will sharpen our awareness of perception. And we never have to leave our own neighborhood to find it.

> Though we travel the world over to find the beautiful, we must carry it with us, or we find it not. The best

of beauty is a finer charm than skill in surfaces, in out-
lines, or rules of art can ever teach, namely a radiation
from the work of art, of human character—a wonderful
expression through stone, or canvas, or musical sound,
of the deepest and simplest attributes of our nature,
and therefore most intelligible at last to those souls
which have these attributes. In the sculptures of the
Greeks, in the masonry of the Romans, and in the pictures of the Tuscan and Venetian masters, the highest
charm is the universal language they speak. A confession
of moral nature, of purity, love and hope breathes from
them all. That which we carry to them, the same we
bring back more fairly illustrated in the memory. The
traveler who visits the Vatican and passes from chamber
to chamber through galleries of statues, vases, sarcoph-
agi and candelabra, through all forms of beauty cut in
the richest materials, is in danger of forgetting the sim-
plicity of the principles out of which they all sprung,
and that they had their origin from thoughts and laws
in his own breast. He studies the technical rules on these
wonderful remains, but forgets that these works were
not always thus constellated; that they are the contributions of many ages and many countries; that each came
out of the solitary workshop of one artist, who toiled
perhaps in ignorance of the existence of other sculpture,
created his work without other models save life, household life, and the sweet and smart of personal relations,
of beating hearts, and meeting eyes; of poverty and necessity and hope and fear. These were his inspirations,
and these are the effects he carries home to your heart
and mind.[2]

The essence of beauty is transient, short-lived, fleeting. It is in the eye of the beholder, relative to the
correlation of things at hand and our mood at any given
moment. It is fairer and better than what we see or
hear. It is born out of the commonplace, household
life, personal relations, beating hearts, meeting eyes,

poverty, necessity, hope, and fear. And, finally, the real celebrating of its presence comes as we recall it in our memory, replaying the old records of our thoughts, gazing at the gallery of pictures with the eye of remembrance, and singing the song that is going on within us, a song to which we listen.

These moments are the pinnacles of our experience, lifting us out of the dreary circumstances and giving us pleasure and delight until we fall back and again become our ordinary selves. They must be interwoven into our daily existence in order to make life endurable and sweet. If we do not train ourselves to receive beauty when it appears before us, our memory bank will be filled with only the products of the mind, the will, the intellect—cold, logical, and calculating—without serenity, heart, humor, or warmth.

As I grow older, I find myself taking reflective trips during the day to recall sounds, pictures, touches, and experiences from my past which were beautiful and intrinsically pleasing. At that moment, they were virtually indescribable. What it was or what it meant could not have been defined in words; nevertheless, the essence of those occasions has glowingly permeated my soul and continues to bring joy as the months and years go by. In that essence, I celebrate. We are not the happiest when our recollections dazzle us with facts and figures. We are the happiest when they bring us peace.

William Stanley Braithwaite, American poet, author, and critic, tells it like it is in his poem *Sic Vita:*

> Heart free, hand free,
> Blue above, brown under,
> All the world to me
> Is a place of wonder.
>
> Sun shine, moon shine,
> Stars, and winds a-blowing,

All into this heart of mine
　　Flowing, flowing, flowing!

Mind free, step free,
　　Days to follow after,
Joys of life sold to me
　　For the price of laughter.

Girl's love, man's love
　　Love of work and duty,
Just a will of God's to prove
　　Beauty, beauty, beauty!

Who can predict what will stir our hearts or move our spirits? Often, it is that which we least expect, hidden within the larger context of something else.

I recall an incident that occurred about twenty years ago which unexpectedly brought me tremendous pleasure. It was an experience which was inconsequential in the overall scheme of things, but one that has, nevertheless, stuck in my consciousness all these years. Whenever I think of it, I always have a pang of nostalgia and tenderness.

When I was with the Dallas Civic Opera Chorus one season, I got to sing with an ensemble for a particular opera. The ensemble work required extra practice, longer hours, additional costume fittings, and so on, all on top of a very hectic choral schedule. I was also working full-time during the day for Mobil. While being in the ensemble brought added recognition and "glamour," it also brought more work. Often, I went to those evening rehearsals already tired from a full day of duties, and therefore, I was occasionally grumpy or out of sorts when I arrived.

One such evening, in early October, the ensemble was instructed to meet in the hotel room of the opera's prompter, a fine musician named Maestro Vasco Naldini, together with stage director Carlo Maestrini.

These gentlemen were going to work with us individually on banging out notes, blocking a bit of staging, and clarifying problem areas in the score. All of us were to gather there on the eighth floor in Maestro Naldini's suite, where there was a piano and adequate room to do simple staging.

Weary from the day, I got in my car and drove to the hotel, wishing I could spend the evening at home in front of the fireplace (had I had one) with a cup of hot tea and a good book. "Why did I ever want to be selected for this group anyway?" I mused. "I'm tired, it's cold, and I don't even feel like singing tonight." But I drove on, parked my car on the street and trudged up to the designated meeting room.

Upon arrival, both Naldini and Maestrini greeted me warmly (as only Italian men can do) with a kiss on each cheek, a few exchanges in Italian, and various comments about the unseasonably cold weather for early October. All very convivial. But it didn't alter my mood.

After a bit, when the ensemble members had arrived, we began to work on the chorus in earnest. Everybody else, amazingly enough, seemed in the same frame of mind as I was. The Dallas Civic Opera Chorus, for the most part, was composed of individuals who worked elsewhere during the day. There were those of us in the business world, teachers, doctors, florists, and others from many different walks of life. So when we got together for rehearsal, it was generally at a time when we had already spent our best hours at our source of livelihood. Most people went home to a leisurely dinner and an evening of watching television or relaxing with family and friends. But those of us in the chorus went on to our second job. It wasn't always easy.

I loved singing in the opera chorus, so much so that

I participated actively in it for fifteen consecutive years. But there were evenings I would have given my right arm to be free of "yet one more rehearsal." This was such an evening, and apparently, from the sounds we produced, everyone else felt the same. Nothing came together. Notes were off pitch or wrong. Attacks and releases were badly timed. Tempers flared. Everybody's biorhythms were out of whack and it seemed no one wanted to be there.

Notwithstanding that fact, everyone's attention had been directed to the ensemble work, even though we were having unfavorable results. Suddenly, with utterly no provocation and in the midst of this psychological malaise, the two gentlemen in charge raised their arms as though on cue, stopping us dead in our vocal tracks. Maestrini wordlessly walked over to the drapes that had been covering a very large, glass picture window and opened them to reveal a spectacular view of millions of twinkling city lights below, as far as one could see on the horizon of that cold, crisp night. He then dimmed the room lights a bit. Naldini, in the meantime, had sat down at the piano and begun to play the soft strains of an Italian love song. Little by little, the two men joined in with the piano, harmonizing in their native language about the joys and sorrows of romance. It was absolutely beautiful! Their voices weren't all that well-trained, but in spite of that, they sang from full hearts of love and fellowship and that moment in time was beautiful for them—and for us who sat there mesmerized, listening.

It lifted everyone of us out of our weary, irritable moods as we were silently transfixed, enjoying the music and looking out at the lights from the city. We loved it! It probably lasted no more than two minutes at the most. Nevertheless, in all its transience, that simple fleeting moment of beauty moved our hearts, made us better than we were, and gave us each something to take with us for the rest of our lives. It even caused us to sing better later as the rehearsal continued. Our spirits were captured, filled with the essence of beauty. And suddenly the weariness of the day no longer mattered.

There is so much beauty around us, if we will only take the time to notice it. You can make a conscious effort to look for the essence and therefore develop an appreciation for the beautiful things in life. Your days will seem a lot less harried, I promise you. Beauty has a way of totally capturing our senses, making us forget the fact that the car stalled on the way to work this morning, that the kids spilled chocolate milk on the carpet, that the workload keeps piling up. For a few brief shining moments, nothing else seems to matter. And the wonderful thing about beauty is that we can store it in our minds to be played over and over again. John Keats captured this idea of looking for the essence in his poem "Endymion":

A thing of beauty is a joy for ever:
Its loveliness increases; it will never
Pass into nothingness; but still will keep
A bower quiet for us, and a sleep
Full of sweet dreams, and health, and quiet breathing.
Therefore, on every morrow, are we wreathing
A flowery band to bind us to the earth,
Spite of despondence, of the inhuman dearth
Of noble natures, of the gloomy days,
Of all the unhealthy and o'er-darkened ways
Made for our searching: yes, in spite of all,
Some shape of beauty moves away the pall
From our dark spirits. Such the sun, the moon,
Trees old and young, sprouting a shady boon
For simple sheep; and such are daffodils

With the green world they live in; and clear rills
That for themselves a cooling covert make
'Gainst the hot season; the mid-forest brake,
Rich with a sprinkling of fair musk-rose blooms:
And such too is the grandeur of the dooms
We have imagined for the mighty dead;
All lovely tales that we have heard or read:
An endless fountain of immortal drink,
Pouring unto us from the heaven's brink.
Nor do we merely feel these essences
For one short hour; no, even as the trees
That whisper round a temple become soon
Dear as the temple's self, so does the moon,
The passion poesy, glories infinite,
Haunt us till they become a cheering light
Unto our souls, and bound to us so fast,
That, whether there be shine, or gloom o'ercast,
They must always be with us, or we die.

There is so much that we take for granted. Our eyes
often pass right over beauty as we are caught up in
the workaholic, get-ahead rat race of life. But if we
*look,* we are sure to find beauty:

- in a breathtaking sunrise or sunset
- in the graceful movements of a dancer
- in the scenery while driving down the interstate
- in a mare nuzzling her colt
- in the wonderful harmony of a concerto
- in the face of a sweetheart, a stranger, a child
- in the stars twinkling on a clear night
- in the costuming and cinematography of a movie
- in the architecture of the Parthenon, the Eiffel
  Tower, or the World Trade Center

- in a single flower blooming next to the sidewalk
- in the squirrels scampering across the front lawn
- in the words of a song, a story, a poem, a love letter

Practice looking for the essence, and celebrate beauty with the awe and respect it is due. A thing of beauty is *indeed* a joy for ever.

# 11
# Celebrating
# America

## SINGING
## HER
## PRAISES

America is a place. I know you know that but I want to point it out anyway because that makes this chapter different from the rest. In chapters 1 through 10 I've talked about celebrating qualities or activities—topics that are rather esoteric in their perceptions. I've said anything I wanted in those chapters because no reader can challenge nor deny what is meaningful to *me*.

However, to write about a place is different, because the places I enjoy may not be the ones you enjoy, for justifiable reasons. We may each "experience" the same place, but in very different ways.

After my first visit to New Orleans I remember telling my parents how they were going to love it there—the history, the architecture, the French Quarter, the food, the music. I ranted on and on about its charms and attractions. On their way to Florida a few months later, they decided to spend one day in New Orleans at my nagging encouragement. It was pouring rain when they arrived. Having no map and being uncertain of exactly how to get to the Quarter, they were tempted to drive right through, but my "you're gonna love it, you're gonna *love* it" kept ringing in their ears. So they stopped at a local service station to inquire the proper directions to Jackson Square. Inching their way along, they finally made it to Royal Street. It was still raining as they circled around, looking for a place to park. Eventually locating an "ideal" spot, they pulled in. They ran in the rain to Antoine's for lunch, only to find it closed for repairs. Irritated, they returned to the car which had, in the meantime, been ticketed because they were in a No Parking zone. Do you think they had fallen in love with New Orleans? Hungry, wet, and disgusted, they thought they'd check out one more place for lunch, then be on their way before things possibly went from bad to worse. As they were backing out of their illegal parking spot they were side-swiped by a passing motorist, who hit them and fled. (Isn't there a Murphy's Law for all this?)

Needless to say, Mother and Dad's impression of New Orleans was vastly different from mine. And I understand why, but I'm sorry to report time never permitted opportunity for them to have a second chance to return (just to see the Vieux Carre, if for no other reason). They never knew the fun and beauty of that marvelous city of tradition, jazz, the Mardi Gras, and international cuisine—one of my favorite cities in America.

Occasionally, I hear people complaining about America and I don't understand. When that happens, I consider them as fightin' words. I put up my dukes. "America is too structured," they say, "too provincial. What does it offer me? The laws are strict and the country is too religious." I've actually heard that! Then they add this parting shot, "I'd like to go to Australia on the next boat." My advice is, *"Go!"* In fact, a poem from the *Wall Street Journal* reiterates my injunction:

### The Dumbest Person In The World

How dumb?
Very dumb.
It's the
American
who knocks
what he's got.
Here's what
he's got:
A country of
unbounded beauty.
Almost unlimited
natural resources.
A judicial system
that is the envy
of the rest of
world.
Food so plentiful
overeating is a
major problem.
A press
nobody can dominate.
A ballot box
nobody can stuff.
Churches of your choice.
One hundred million jobs.
Freedom to go anywhere

> you want, with the
> planes, cars and highways
> to get you there.
> Social Security.
> Medicare.
> Unemployment insurance.
> Public schools and
> plentiful scholarships.
> Opportunity to become a
> millionaire.
> OK, Complainer,
> what's your
> second
> choice?
> Go.[1]

There is no place on earth like America, and even the complainer knows that's true.

The face of America is unusually beautiful. All one needs to do to recognize this fact is travel—over the mountains and deserts of the West, across the Great Central Plains, through the National Parks, down our wide rivers. In the natural contours of hills, rocks, valleys, water, and landscape, one is overwhelmed by the harmony and colorful richness which covers our land. God has created *magnificent* beauty in the physical face of America.

American ingenuity has only enhanced that beauty. Each time I fly into Los Angeles I am amazed at the expanse of rooftops, twinkling lights, and vegetation which stretch as far as the eye can see. Even as the land merges with the Pacific Ocean, there is contour and beauty.

I confess I am a city slicker more than a country dweller. I even like the freeways! I find tremendous joy in visiting a city in which I've never been, attempting to pick up that unique flavor which each city has.

I like to check out the downtown area, walk the streets, observe the architecture, and shop in the stores. If time permits, I visit art museums, hear the symphony, or go to a play. The size and quality of the local library also says a lot about a city. I want to "taste" its culture—its flavor. In short, I want to absorb all the traditions, sights, and sounds which America has to offer from its storehouse of natural luxuries and man-made contributions. Poet Walt Whitman expresses it in this way:

> I hear America singing,
>     the varied carols I hear . . .
> Singing with open mouths
>     their strong melodious songs.[2]

As a college student, I read the autobiographical account of the famous American architect, Frank Lloyd Wright, who believed the natural contours of the earth should blend inherently with man-made structures. "Organic architecture," he called it. "No house should ever be *on* any hill," he said, "or on anything. It should be *of* the hill, belonging to it, so hill and house could live together each the happier for the other." I love that concept! It emphasizes the fact that beauty is not just in the countenance of something. Beauty is in the *physiognomy*—in the expression and character of what makes up the beauty. America's beauty is not only in its features; its beauty is in the character underneath those features.

America is more than a place. America is a spirit, and the spirit of any place comes from its people. The American people—we're a wonderful lot! Being an American fills me with a tremendous sense of pride and gratitude. I'm proud of our rugged individualism. I'm proud of our curiosity and love of novelty which

permits unlimited opportunity for creativity. I'm proud
of our generosity and openhandedness to other nations.
I'm proud of our support of one another. And, I'm
grateful that as a nation we value a person more than
a principle, that we enjoy so many freedoms, that we're
not afraid to be forthright and daring. I'm grateful that
we are friendly and warm, that we can laugh at ourselves, and that in our youth we respect age.

And I patriotically love our Pledge of Allegience and
National Anthem. I can't get through either one without crying because of what each conveys.

Picture this—it actually happened: I was sitting on
a pier on the Greek island of Mykonos early one summer vacation morning, thousands of miles away from
home, eating breakfast—fresh strawberries in cream
and a cup of Greek coffee. Suddenly, unannounced,
out of nowhere there came the faint strains of a band
playing our National Anthem. "Oh say can you see
by the dawn's early light, what so proudly. . . ." I
couldn't believe my ears. I stopped chewing, listened,
swallowed, automatically rose to my feet and I put my
hand over my heart. After a bit, I began to sing, then
to cry. I thought maybe it was God's angels engaged
in a novel way to call me home—either to the U.S.A.
or heaven—only to find out later that an American
naval vessel had docked in the harbor the night before
and their band played the "Star-Spangled Banner" on
deck each morning. From then on, I eagerly anticipated hearing the American National Anthem on that
Greek island at precisely ten o'clock each morning.
And each morning I cried. It was the spirit of America
that met me on foreign soil for the rest of my vacation.

Didn't the 1984 Olympics take on new meaning
when the torch bearer ran through your town or your
neighborhood? Weren't you there with your camera?
I was . . . yelling, applauding, and crying. I'm a sucker

for patriotism every time—and proud of it. I celebrate it. I sing its praises.

Theodore Roosevelt once said:

> There can be no fifty-fifty Americanism
> in this country.
> There is room here for only hundred percent
> Americanism.

It's the people who *love* America who have the right and the power to make our country what we want it to be—ordinary, everyday, garden-variety people. It's the people who are born here or who immigrate here from other nations. In the early seventies, the *New York Times* printed an editorial by a Polish immigrant named Janina Atkins who had come here six years earlier with $2.60 in her purse, some clothes, a bundle of old letters, and a few books, hoping for a new life and happiness in a strange country. She spoke of something in the air of America that filled her soul with a feeling of independence—an independence which begot strength. She talked of believing in the future, and the future did not disappoint her. She wrote,

> Today . . . my husband is studying for his doctorate. We live in a comfortable apartment in mid-Manhattan. Weekends we drive to the country. . . .
>
> I love this country because when I want to move from one place to another I do not have to ask permission. Because when I want to go abroad I just buy a ticket and go.
>
> I love America because when I need a needle I go to the nearest Woolworths. . . . I love it because I do not have to stand in line for hours to buy a piece of tough, fat meat. I love it because, even with inflation, I do not have to pay a day's earnings for a small chicken.

I love America because America trusts me. When I go into a shop to buy a pair of shoes I am not asked to produce my identity card. I love it because my mail is not censored. My phone is not tapped. My conversation with friends is not reported to the secret police.

Sometimes when I walk with my husband through the streets of New York, all of a sudden we stop, look at each other and smile and kiss. People think we are in love, and it is true. But we are also in love with America . . . standing in the street, amidst the noise and pollution, we suddenly realize what luck and joy it is to live in a free country.[3]

That touching story is wonderful. It causes me once again to count the innumerable blessings that are mine in this great country. It reminds me that no one has a corner on making America what it is. That inalienable right to build into its quality of excellence is the prerogative of *every* person. Everything that grows comes out of people. In the words of our major prophet, Walt Whitman:

> Everything comes out of the dirt—
> everything; everything comes out of the
> people, everyday people, the people as you
> find them and leave them; people, people,
> just people![4]

When we get down in the dirt, we find that that's where the seeds are planted, dreams are watered, ideas are cultivated, and growth occurs. It starts with people. It can start with me. It can start with you.

America is a place. America is a spirit. America is also a future. I hear a lot of gloom about our nation and I recognize its source. There is certainly reason for concern. Our newspapers and periodicals are filled with tragic stories about people who never progress out of the dirt into which they were born, living their lives with maladaptive behavior. The possibilities of nuclear holocaust hang heavy upon our horizons. There are pollution problems which plague our environment. The computer craze has nullified the caring workplace. I see this. I read these narratives. But I do not believe we have to live in the oppressive shadows of these sleeping giants. There will always be unregenerate persons, violence, failure, ignorance, fear—that is the nature of fallen humanity. There is not a country on the face of the earth that does not have its periods of progression and retrogression. Nevertheless, in the long-range view, in spite of the complex strains of life, our future is exciting. And here's the reason: we have a magnificent heritage.

Our country was established by God-fearing men and women, those who declared "that all men are created equal; that they are endowed by their Creator with certain inalienable rights; that among these are life, liberty, and the pursuit of happiness." Our forefathers believed in liberty and justice for all, a creed which has made our nation a forerunner and strong advocate of freedom the world over.

Olympic runner Kip Mibey from Kenya recently completed a run from Santa Monica, California, to the Statue of Liberty in New York to thank Americans for their help in feeding his African countrymen. In a letter he said, "I ask myself what makes America. . . . Is it because they are still maintaining democracy, or because they are, as they say, a 'melting pot'? But I concluded that she is great because she is 'one nation under God.'"

May we never lose our passion for the inalienable rights of men. And may we never, *ever* fail to live

up to our motto, "In God We Trust." Those are the
very foundations on which this country was founded,
and without them we would surely fall.

As we consider all that our nation has accumulated
from its European forefathers, progressing and increas-
ing in abundance and transmission, century after century, in the field of the arts, technology, medicine,
philosophy, invention, and education, there should be
no end to the songs of praise we sing for this foundation
upon which we continue to build and grow. And no
one sings it better than Walt Whitman:

> One song, America, before I go,
> I'd sing, o'er all the rest, with trumpet sound,
> For thee—the Future.
>
> I'd sow a seed for thee of endless Nationality;
> I'd fashion thy Ensemble, including Body and Soul;
> I'd show, away ahead, the real Union, and
>     how it may be accomplish'd. . . .
>
> Belief I sign—and Preparation;
> As Life and Nature are not great with reference
>     to the Present only,
> But greater still from what is to come,
> Out of that formula for Thee I sing.[5]

# Benediction

## THE
## CELEBRATION
## OF GOD

Often, when we consider what God is like, the picture in our mind scares us away. We envision an over-powering Being, much too big or imposing to be interested in our "little" problems. Or perhaps we see God as too busy to hear us or be aware of our needs. In the mind of some, there is no imagination at all of what He is like.

A mother in Bartonville, Illinois, tells the story of her daughter who was busy painting a portrait that she claimed was of God. When the mother pointed out that nobody knew what God looked like, the child said, "They will when I'm finished."

That's great! Everybody must draw his or her own perception of God. We must each have an object of trust and worship. It is imperative for our longing hearts, which find complete satisfaction and peace only in the God who made us. He is the ultimate celebration! Psalm 57:7–11 proclaims:

> My heart is steadfast, O God,
>   my heart is steadfast!
> I will sing and make melody!
>   Awake, my soul!
> Awake; O harp and lyre!
>   I will awake the dawn!
> I will give thanks to thee, O Lord, among the peoples;
>   I will sing praises to thee among the nations.
> For thy steadfast love is great to the heavens,
>   thy faithfulness to the clouds.
>
> Be exalted, O God, above the heavens!
>   Let thy glory be over all the earth! (RSV)

The wisdom and doctrine of Scripture teach that the experience of celebrating God is the core of worship. It is the quintessence of praise and thanksgiving— the most perfect manifestation of a heart that gratefully fellowships with the One who provides life and all the gifts of living. In fact, a grateful heart is not only the greatest virtue, it is the seedbed for all other virtues. When we are caught up in the celebration of God there is neither room nor time for the invasion of negative living. As we rejoice before the Lord, as we serve Him in the area of our calling, as we enter into the love that surrounds our days, as we give thanks to Him for His kindness and faithfulness, we celebrate God.

Counting our blessings gives birth to that celebration. It cannot fail. In the words of Christina Rossetti:

> Were there no God, we would be in this glorious world with grateful hearts: and no one to thank.[1]

All of the topics of celebration addressed in this book diminish by comparison as we enter into and benefit from a personal relationship with God through His Son, Jesus Christ—as we celebrate His attributes. God is the One who enables us to savor the moment and grow older joyfully. He provides camaraderie and intimacy through friends and families. No reunion is possible without His arrangement, timing, and protection. He infiltrates the workplace, making it an enjoyable part of living rather than a task to get through hurriedly so we can move on to better things. Our accomplishments are enhanced by knowing we have His approval and are made possible only because He gave us the dream in the first place. It is He who intensifies imagination, beauty, and knowledge. And every day, in our vast country, we see and experience His handiwork in blessings, provisions, and grace. A relationship with Him enlarges life. It is the reason for celebrating anything.

> May God grant to us a hunger for Him which will cause us to pursue Him in worship as a way of life . . . a hunger which will drive us to closer fellowship with His people. This will result in a rich corporate worship experience, characterized by unity, sensitivity, and understanding. . . . In loving God with our whole being we will love what He loves, hate what He hates, and long to see His purposes carried out through us!
> Let us celebrate God![2]

When we're finished painting our portrait of God, the people with whom we come in contact should know what He looks like. There should be no question in their minds because they'll see Him as He is—the ultimate object of celebration.

Let's throw a party in celebration of Him. Let's thank Him for who we are, and what we are, and where we are. Come with a joyful heart, ready to have the time of your life. I'll bring the streamers—you bring the confetti!

# NOTES

**Chapter 1**
1. Ann Wells, *Los Angeles Times,* 14 April 1985.

**Chapter 2**
1. Sophia Loren, *Women and Beauty* (London: William Morrow and Co., Inc., 1984), 206.
2. E. E. Cummings, in a letter written in 1955.
3. Sophia Loren, *Women and Beauty,* 218.

**Chapter 3**
1. Wolfgang Puck, *Modern French Cooking for the American Kitchen* (Boston Houghton Mifflin Co., 1981), xv.

**Chapter 4**
1. Gail Sheehy, *Pathfinders* (New York: William Morrow and Co., Inc., 1981), 186.
2. Barbara Walters, *How to Talk with Practically Anybody about Practically Anything* (New York: Dell Publishing Co., Inc., 1979), 142.

**Chapter 5**
1. Emma Lazarus, "The Great Colossus."
2. Dietrich Bonhoeffer, *Listen to Love: Reflections on the Seasons of the Year* (New York: Regina Press, 1968), 248.

**Chapter 6**
1. William Brighty Rands (Matthew Browne), *The Child's World.*
2. Richard N. Bolles, *The Three Boxes of Life* (Berkeley, CA: Ten Speed Press, 1981), 118.
3. Terence H. White, *The Once and Future King* (New York: C. P. Putnam's Sons, 1958).
4. Shearson Lehman/American Express, Inc., 1984 Advertisement (New York: *Business Week* magazine, 11 June 1984), 74–75.
5. John Gruen, *The Private World of Leonard Bernstein* (New York: Viking Press, 1968), 154.

**Chapter 7**
1. Thomas J. Peters and Robert H. Waterman, Jr., *In Search of Excellence* (New York: Warner Books, 1984), 277.
2. John Naisbitt and Patricia Aburdene, *Re-Inventing the Corporation* (New York: Warner Books, 1985), 4–5.
3. Robert Updegraff, "The Long Journey," as published in *Successful Supervisor* (Chicago: Dartnell, 29 July 1985), 2.

**Chapter 8**
1. *Newsweek* magazine, 10 March 1986, 34.
2. Robert Schuller, *The Be-Happy Attitudes* (Waco, TX: Word, Inc., 1985), 119.

**Chapter 9**
1. Leo Buscaglia, *Bus 9 to Paradise* (Thorofare, NJ: Slack, Inc., 1986), 172–3.

**Chapter 10**
1. From "Alchemy," by Francis Carlin, as published in *Anthology of Catholic Poets*, Joyce Kilmer, ed. (New York: Halcyon House, 1940), 303.
2. From "Art," *The Essays of Ralph Waldo Emerson* (New York: The Heritage Press, 1934), 142.

**Chapter 11**
1. As published in *The Wall Street Journal* by United Technologies Corporation, Hartford, CT.
2. From "I Hear America Singing," by Walt Whitman, *Leaves of Grass* (The Easton Press, 1977), 10.
3. Robert Flood, ed., *America, God Shed His Grace on Thee* (Chicago: Moody Press, 1975), 12.
4. *Modern Minds* (Lexington, MA: D. C. Heath and Co.), 210.
5. From "One Song, America, Before I Go," by Walt Whitman, *Leaves of Grass*, 507.

**Benediction**
1. Christina Rosetti, as published in *The Encyclopedia of Religious Quotations*, Frank S. Mead, ed., (Old Tappan, NJ: Fleming H. Revell Co.), 440.

2. Ronald B. Allen et al, *Worship: Rediscovering the Missing Jewel* (Portland, OR: Multnomah, 1982), 190.